Teaching with Story

Other August House books
by Margaret Read MacDonald:

Conejito

Earth Care

Fat Cat

Five-Minute Tales

Ghost Stories from the Pacific Northwest

Go to Sleep, Gecko

Great Smelly, Slobbery Small-Tooth Dog

Old Woman Who Lived In a Vinegar Bottle

Parents' Guide to Storytelling

Peace Tales

Round Book

Shake-It-Up Tales

Storyteller's Start-Up Book

Surf War!

Three-Minute Tales

Tuck-Me-In Tales

Teaching with Story
Classroom Connections to Storytelling

Margaret Read MacDonald,
Jennifer MacDonald Whitman,
and Nathaniel Forrest Whitman

AUGUST HOUSE

Published 2013
by August House, Inc.

Atlanta, Georgia
augusthouse.com

ISBN 978-1-939160-72-0

Cover design by Graham Anthony
Book design by H. K. Stewart

Manufactured in the United States
10 9 8 7 6 5 4 3 2 1

Library of Congress Cataloging-in-Publication Data

MacDonald, Margaret Read, 1940-
 Teaching with story : classroom connections to storytelling / by Margaret Read MacDonald,
Jennifer MacDonald Whitman, and Nathaniel Forrest Whitman.
     pages cm
 Includes bibliographical references and index.
 ISBN 978-1-939160-72-0 (alk. paper)
 1. Storytelling. 2. Teaching. I. Title.
 LB1042.M234 2013
 372.67'7--dc23
                              2013013873

Printed in the United States of America
This book is printed on archival-quality paper that meets requirements of the American
National Standard for Information Sciences, Permanence of Paper, Printed Library Materials,
ANSI Z39.48-1984.

To all teachers everywhere, who get up at dawn and rush out to make a home in their classrooms, a nest where students can be nurtured and taught. May story make your teaching easier—and your days more joyful.

—MRM

To all students everywhere, whose joy and delight in learning make us better teachers. May you share your own stories confidently with the world. And to Cordelia—the hero of our hearts. We cherish your unfolding story.

—JMW and NFW

Table of Contents

Introduction

I have learned…that the head does not hear anything until the heart has listened, and what the heart knows today, the head will understand tomorrow.

—James Stephens, *The Crock of Gold*

What Is Storytelling?

Storytelling is the act of using the human voice to share a story with an audience. Telling a story is not the same thing as reciting a monologue or a poem. The words are not memorized, so they are not static. Storytellers take their cues from their listeners and adapt their stories as they tell, adding an embellishment here, slowing the pace there, as they tailor the story for the needs of a particular audience. The listeners also have an important job: They need to create their own images and respond in the moment as they hear the tale unfold. This is exactly how we see storytelling functioning in the classroom—the human voice breathes life into a narrative and sparks the imagination of the listener.

Our Team

We are a family of storytellers and we each bring to the table a unique perspective on using stories in schools. Margaret has been teaching storytelling classes to teachers and school librarians for several decades and she has received enthusiastic feedback over the years about how storytelling has enhanced instruction for teachers around the globe. Jen has been an Early Childhood teacher for fifteen years and uses storytelling throughout the year and across the curriculum in her own classroom. Nat used storytelling as a classroom teacher and now has shifted to the role of school librarian. He brings his experience using stories with students in the school library setting. In our family conversations about the importance of storytelling, we believed there needed to be a book like this to outline the benefits of storytelling in the classroom and to give teachers quick and easy stories to tell right away. You will hear our different voices throughout the book.

Once Upon A Time:
Storytelling as a Teaching Technique

*Once upon a time…*the moment those words are spoken, you know that you are on a magical journey. You can't anticipate the destination, but you can be sure that you are in for an enjoyable trip.

When teachers first begin using storytelling in the classroom, many express amazement at how effectively stories can be used to excite students and connect them with new ideas. Yet, this is not surprising when we consider that oral storytelling has been valued throughout history as a vital way to cement information and societal expectations in the minds of listeners, both young and old. Humans have used stories to educate from the very beginning.

Stories not only teach, but they also create community. When you look into the eyes of your students and begin to share a story, magic happens. You are building a bridge between yourself as the teller and your students as the listeners. You can see this instantly in the way your students lean forward and their eyes sparkle. Telling stories in the classroom brings us closer to one another and helps us understand our common humanity together. Storytelling delivers emotion, information, culture, and language in a package that nothing else can approach.

Why is storytelling so effective? The eye-to-eye contact and the intense personal relationship with the storyteller convey the story directly to the heart of the listener.

The discreet shape of the story and its elegant format encourage close attention. This is not just more talk—this is an event. There is a beginning. There is an ending coming soon. Attention must be paid.

And within the story event something exciting is happening. Layers of motifs and information surface through a story. Folktales have been told and retold for generations. Like a pebble rolled and rolled over time in a stream, they come down to us perfectly smoothed and shaped to fit our human minds. They fulfill certain emotional needs. They engage the listener. And they are memorable.

Information wrapped in a story enters the mind and sticks. Using a story to introduce a topic creates a momentum for information that is to come.

Sometimes, in our busy, high-tech world, we forget the value of the simple act of sharing a story. Students crave stories, and when we slow down and share a tale with them, they are grateful beyond measure. We hope to convince you that taking a moment out to tell a story is a gift you give your students—and yourself!

You will be amazed to find how story bonds your students into a more cohesive classroom. And a well-chosen story can function throughout the year to set expectations and serve as a valuable reference point for you and your students.

Stories bring their own positive energy into your classroom. Once you've shared a story, don't let it go! Students love to play with tales and to revisit them in different ways. Some stories become class favorites and are asked for again and again.

There are a thousand reasons to tell stories in the classroom, but really, the most important reason for bringing storytelling into your classroom is joy. Once you begin a tradition of storytelling with your students you will find that you delight in the telling as much as your students delight in listening.

We hope to convince you that storytelling is a teaching technique you cannot live without. Telling stories is as simple as finding a great tale you love, taking it into your heart, and opening your mouth to pass it along!

I was astounded by the look in their eyes as they watched my every movement and listened to each word as though I was a famous magician ready to pull a rabbit from my hat. It felt a little uncomfortable and magical at the same time. I was afraid that the spell would break at any moment. When I finished my first real storytelling debut I was amazed at how well my students responded and more dumbfounded that I actually remember the story. It was a moment in my teaching career that I will always remember, one that I will never forget. I am a storyteller!

— Peggy Barnes, Grade 2, Sunrise Elementary, Spokane, WA

The Seven C's of Storytelling: Using this Book.

Storytelling can enliven learning in your classroom throughout the day, every day of the year. As we were organizing our thoughts about the benefits of storytelling, "C" words kept popping up in our conversations: Cooperation—Communication—Character. As we carried on with our brainstorming we realized that telling stories across the Seven C's was the perfect metaphor for what we are encouraging you to do with story. A good story can take you anywhere around the world and back again. So we've organized what we perceive as the primary benefits of storytelling into "The Seven C's" of storytelling in the classroom. We will show you ways that storytelling can be used to enrich your classroom in relation to Community, Character, Communication, Curriculum, Cultural Connections, Creativity and Confidence.

One chapter is devoted to each "C" and includes two stories with suggestions for extending the stories beyond the telling. The tales included in this book are all easy to learn and fun to tell. These are the "grand slam" stories that never fail us. They are tales that we have told extensively with classes around the world and that children have responded to with enthusiasm consistently. We hope you select a few of the stories that appeal to you most and find your own ways to use them across the curriculum.

Most tales can be used easily to support all of the Seven C's. To illustrate this, we'll start the book with a favorite tale about Grandfather Bear and Chipmunk. We'll then revisit this story in each section of the book to show how one short story can be used to enhance your teaching in myriad ways. Look for this "Grandfather Bear Connection" at the end of each chapter.

After we have examined the Seven C's, we will talk about the power of using storytelling in second language learning, an area in which storytelling is especially useful. Then we will share experiences of those who have used storytelling successfully with special needs populations.

Later in the book, we will talk in more detail about learning and performing stories. We'll give a few simple tips for learning a new story quickly. We want you to think of this as a natural and simple affair. There is nothing to stress about; storytelling is something you do because it is fun!

Finally, we will note how storytelling can help you meet the standards and benchmarks in your school system. In our rush to improve student learning and with the range of pressures that have been put on teachers through high-stakes testing, you might feel that there is no time for storytelling. At the end of the book, you will find a resource section that addresses these concerns. We will use the Common Core standards as a guide and we will highlight the direct links that storytelling has with many of the standards we are already trying to reach. If someone ever questions the fact that you are spending time telling tales, you can explain how many different standards you are addressing every time you tell a story.

Need more proof? We also include information about current research on the value of storytelling in the classroom. Then you'll be able to share with your colleagues that really there's no excuse for not including storytelling in your day, every day!

Throughout the book, we've included quotations from teachers who have taken Margaret's storytelling classes over the years. These quotes highlight the power of storytelling in a variety of classroom settings from the perspectives of teachers who have used stories successfully with their own students for a range of purposes.

We love the stories included in this book and hope you will too, but these are only the tip of the iceberg. There is an entire world of delightful stories out there for you to discover. At the very end of the book, you'll find a lengthy resource section to help you delve further into the wonderful world of story to find your own personal favorites.

But for now, a simple tale!

Grandfather Bear Is Hungry
An *Even* Folktale from Siberia

Grandfather Bear woke up one fine spring morning.
He came out of his cave. He had been sleeping all winter.
"I am SO hungry!" said Grandfather Bear. "I am SO hungry!"
Grandfather Bear went to the berry patch to look for blackberries.
He looked and looked.
But it was too early in the spring. The berries were not ripe yet.

"I am SO hungry!" said Grandfather Bear. "I am SO hungry!"

Grandfather Bear went to the stream to look for salmon.
He looked and looked.
But it was too early in the spring. The salmon were not running yet.

"I am SO hungry!" said Grandfather Bear. "I am SO hungry!"

Grandfather Bear went to a rotten stump. He thought he would find bugs and grubs.
Grandfather Bear began to rake and scrape at that rotten stump.

That stump was the home of Little Chipmunk! He felt his house shaking and quaking!

"Grandfather Bear! Grandfather Bear! What are you DOING! Don't tear my house apart!"

"I am SO hungry!" said Grandfather Bear. "I am SO hungry!"

"Grandfather Bear, I have nuts and dried berries I saved for the winter. I will SHARE with you."

Chipmunk ran down in his hole and filled his cheeks with nuts and berries.
He ran back to the top. "Here, Grandfather Bear!"

"Thank you Little Chipmunk. But I am STILL hungry!"

"Wait, Grandfather Bear. I have more."
Chipmunk ran down. He filled his cheeks and ran up again.
"Here Grandfather Bear!"

"Thank you Little Chipmunk. But I am STILL hungry!"

"Just a moment, Grandfather Bear." All day, Chipmunk ran.
Down and up. Down and up. Down and up.

At last Grandfather Bear was FULL.
"Thank you Little Chipmunk! I want to give you a reward. Stand very still."

Grandfather Bear stroked his heavy claw SO gently…right down Chipmunk's back.
He left five black stripes!
"Now when anyone sees your stripes they will remember…
How kind you were to share with Grandfather Bear."

If you like this story, share it now! Don't wait to read the rest of this book. There is really no necessary *technique* to storytelling. Just take a tale in, then open your mouth and let it come out!

Shortcut to Story Learning

1. Read "Grandfather Bear is Hungry."

2. Read the story out loud. Have fun with Grandfather Bear's "I'm SO HUNGRY!"

3. Stand up and pretend you are Grandfather Bear. Walk around the room telling his story. Then run up and down as Chipmunk and tell his part of the story. This is good exercise.

4. Now see if you can tell the whole story without looking at the text. It doesn't matter what words you use. Just tell what happened. But remember to end with "when people see your stripes, Chipmunk, they will remember how kind you were to share with Grandfather Bear."

5. Tell the story to your class. Don't worry about forgetting or getting things wrong. This is a *folktale*. You are one of the *folk*. Any way you tell this story is just fine. Relax and have fun with it!

I told this short story to my 65-member concert band at school. We had a few minutes of waiting before the bell and I asked them casually, "Would you like to hear a story?" They all answered "YES!" with great energy. I prepared them for a fast story and to listen quickly. They dove in and were enthusiastic for the short sound-bite-like story. The final bell of the day sounded just as I was finishing; the students remained engaged and listened to the moral of the story and they laughed with appreciation at the end when I showed them, "…how the chipmunk got his little black stripes…because he was kind to grandpa bear." The simple concept of "kindness" was well received by all of the band students. Since then, I have reminded students of their social responsibility to be kind and be looking out for the best interest of others, even if there are ill-feelings among people in the group.

—Ryan Lewis, Cedarcrest High School, Duvall, WA.

Part I:
Storytelling across the Curriculum

Chapter 1: COMMUNITY—
Building Community in Your Classroom
Through Storytelling

Their story, yours and mine—it's what we all carry with us on this trip
we take, and we owe it to each other to respect our stories and learn
from them.

— William Carlos Williams

Story brings magic into the classroom. The moment you open your mouth to share a story, the atmosphere changes and students are transformed. The children's eyes open wider, their bodies lean forward, they become physically and mentally engaged in the story. Everyone is linked together in the moment, sharing the same story experience. While you are telling and the students are visualizing, you are co-creating the story together. As students journey with you and create the story in their imaginations, you are also creating a strong sense of community.

Once you have shared a story with your students, it immediately becomes part of your classroom culture. From that day on, the story is a common reference point for the entire class. You and your students will make connections to the story throughout the year. For example, when Jen's students are moving like molasses during a transition time, all she has to say is, "If you ever have to move…" and all of the children chime in, "Move FAST!" They instantly recall the tale of "Mabela the Clever" (found at the end of this chapter) who escaped the cat by moving quickly. When it's time for lunch, she begins saying, "I'm so hungry…" and the students join in with, "I'm so HUNGRY, I'm SOOOO HUNGRY!" and remember Grandfather Bear. Everyone has a giggle and another shared moment with story has helped strengthen the class bond as a community.

Communities have always been defined by stories, be it a religious community, a successful corporation or a classroom. Community stories are cables of shared emotional experience, bound and woven, defining and gathering a community together.

Storytelling is so useful for building community because you know the students and you know the story. You can adapt the tale to meet the needs of your group, aiming parts at those who need it most, emphasizing the pieces you want to bring to your group, and tailoring the whole just for your listeners. There is an anecdote of a rural village where a

TV was brought in for the first time. For a few weeks people flocked to sit in front of it. Then one day the district organizer came and found that no one was watching the TV anymore. Instead they had gone to listen to the village storyteller. "Why aren't you watching the TV I brought you?" he wanted to know. "It can open a window on the world for you!" "Well…" said the villagers, "The TV knows many things, but the storyteller knows us." This transactional experience between teller and audience is what sets storytelling apart. The audience, the teller, and the story intersect to form a clear channel of delight, wonder, and interactive communication.

I've learned I can wake them up with a lively, active story or calm them down with a quiet gentle piece. I can emphasize different elements of stories for the specific needs of my group.

— Kathy McConnell, Grade 1, Dorothy Fox Elementary, Camas, WA

Starting on a High Note: Beginning the School Year with Stories

The start of the school year is all about building community. Storytelling can help you set the tone, vision, and purpose for your classroom. We have certain stories that we tell every year in the first days of school because they allow us to talk about important elements for developing our community of learners. The simple act of sharing a storytelling event in itself creates a bond among the listeners. Together the students share in the emotional ups and downs of the tale's characters. Together they playfully join in the tale's chants, songs, and refrains. At the tale's end the class emerges more bonded, with common reference points to share throughout the coming year of learning together. Sharing tales helps us meld into a learning community, ready to work as a group. We now share a common past through our adventures in story, and we are ready to move forward together for our future. We have laughed together, felt sad together. We are beginning to be a family.

The first week of school is a good time to introduce tales that you would like to refer to throughout the school year. Traditional tales are an amazingly effective tool for sparking discussions about the kind of behavior your students plan to expect of each other throughout the year, so get those tales on board at the very beginning!

One teacher found the folktale "Not Our Problem" (p. 29) fit exactly one of her classroom needs. This is the tale of a ruler who insists that everything that occurs is "not our problem"—until a mounting series of events results in disaster. The first week of school her first graders had thrown trash all over under their lunchroom table. When she asked them to pick things up they all squirmed and said, "I didn't do it." "Back to the classroom!" she commanded. There she sat them down and told them the story of the ruler who denied all responsibility. "Now why did I just tell you this story?" They all got the point. And for the rest of the school year, whenever she saw someone refusing to take responsibility for an action she simply had to say, "Not our problem?" And the point was made.

I love to tell a variety of stories at the beginning of the year…Because the stories are so engaging and easy for students to retell and remember, I can draw upon them over and over throughout the year. When I teach making inferences, I can say, "What do you think the Old Woman might do next time a fairy grants her a wish?" These stories work to discuss cause and effect, compare and contrast, author's purpose, main idea, details, etc. It is wonderful because all the students instantly recall the stories.

—Tammie Enders, Glenwood Elementary, Snohomish, WA

Pressing the Re-Set Button

Storytelling is a powerful tool to use throughout the year with your classroom community. We all have days as teachers when it feels like nothing is working the way we'd planned. On those days when we're feeling frazzled or when the children are particularly unfocused, we turn to a story. A quick story energizes the whole community. It acts as a re-set button. We share a story together, sense the magic of our learning community once more, and then we are ready to move on with the day productively.

The told story is a remarkable way to pull the class together. During the telling every student is fixated on just one thing—the story. For five to ten minutes every student is in the same place mentally and emotionally. Teachers often are amazed at this power of story. "They were all on task!" Of course, they were in the story.

There are about seven students in my class who are consistently off-task. Anything engaging, heartfelt, and memorable is a welcome addition to my teaching repertoire. Storytelling is the perfect way to teach things like fairness, kindness, respect, and consideration.

— Allen Storkel, Springbrook Elementary, Kent, WA.

Honoring Each Child's Tradition

Our schools bring children from many cultural backgrounds together. Purposefully sharing folktales from the cultural traditions of each of your students is a wonderful way to honor each child in your classroom community. For more on this see Chapter 6, Cultural Connections. One good way to honor those students who speak different languages is to share a story with some of their language incorporated. In Chapter 8 we show ways to incorporate tales into your classroom via translation.

Hearing Each Child's Story

An important part of developing our classroom community throughout the year is making sure we hear the voices of all of our students. As the year progresses, make sure that each child has a chance to speak and be heard. They may share folktales they have learned, or they may share stories from their own experiences. Each child needs to be honored through the active listening of the whole class. The act of careful listening is a gift to the speaker. Hearing each other's stories and honoring each other in this way builds community.

Welcoming New Students

Sharing stories on the days new students join your classroom can help welcome them into the group. The bonding moment of a shared story embraces new students and helps them feel a part of the classroom community.

The community building was apparent to me when I got a new student. My students were singing and patting their legs, uninhibited about how they looked to each other and just enjoying the story. I noticed my new student looking around unsure of what to do, when one of my students leaned over and said, "Mrs. Lavine tells the best stories." My new student joined right in as well.

— Angie Lavine, Grade 4, Kent Elementary, Kent, WA

Resolving Conflict Through Story

In order to maintain a productive classroom community throughout the year, we all guide our students to resolve conflicts calmly and independently when they arise. A well-chosen story can help create a more congenial atmosphere in your classroom. Share stories of friends who work their problems out in a friendly way, like "How to Break a Bad Habit" (p. 143), as a starting point for discussions about how friends will treat each other in your classroom community.

Jennifer Hulbert used a story of quarreling goats, "Two Goats on a Bridge" (p. 162), to help two students resolve their conflict.

Today after lunch, I had a couple of students complaining about things that had happened on the playground at recess, so after listening to the students, I told "Two Goats on a Bridge." I had the students pick a partner and practice. I had them switch partners two times, and I made sure the students who were having problems were partners one time. When I walked by them, they were laughing together, not even remembering what had happened at recess.

— Jennifer Hulbert, Grade 2, William Wright Elementary, Las Vegas, Nevada

In Time of Emergency a Story Can Calm

Let's hope you don't need to use stories in this way, but teachers have found that a pocketful of stories can be invaluable when you are responsible for your students in times of crisis.

We had a lock-down today and numerous SWAT teams came to our building. We could hear the helicopter above us. The students were nervous so I decided to tell them some stories. They seemed to enjoy them and it helped to keep them calm. It was a crazy and stressful day but the storytelling made it a bit more bearable.

— Rita Lenes, Grade 1, Carriage Crest Elementary, Kent, Washington

On September 11, 2001 teachers were searching for ways to calm themselves and their students. One teacher wrote: "Telling stories helped the kids and me keep our minds off the fear and confusion of the day. I was grateful for having this resource of stories."

Leann Onishi looked for stories to calm both herself and her students.
I really searched for stories for comfort for myself this week. There is something special about a message of wisdom that isn't preachy, about being able to rely on the rhythm and repetition of familiar words to give life meaning and structure when the world around you seems unsettled. I went home and read Peace Tales, searching for a story I could offer kids or adults as a gift to help them sort their thoughts.

—Leann Onishi, Cedar Way Elementary, Lynwood, WA

We hope you will find many tales which help you shape a positive classroom community and that you continue to use them for years to come.

Let's Look at Grandfather Bear

"Grandfather Bear" is a lovely tale to use with students early in the year. Grandfather Bear and Chipmunk serve as the perfect role models for what we expect in the classroom. We are all there to help one another with our learning. When we work together and share resources, we all benefit.

A kindergarten teacher told, "Grandfather Bear is Hungry" during the first week of class. Then for the rest of the school year, whenever she saw a student sharing, she would quietly go over and gently give the child a stroke down the back. Everyone knew that this was recognition for sharing behavior.

Try a Tale!

Here are two of our favorite beginning-of-year stories: "Mabela the Clever" is a tale that Jen uses every first day of school with her students. It's great for primary classes. Mabela's father gives excellent advice that could serve as classroom agreements for the year. "Keep your ears open and listen. Keep your eyes open and look. When you speak, pay attention to what you are saying. When you have to move, move FAST." We also include a slightly more mature tale, "Not Our Problem," which is useful for every age level from kindergarten to adult.

Mabela the Clever
Based on a Limba Folktale from Sierra Leone

In the early times some were clever and some were foolish.
The Cat was one of the clever ones. The Mice were mostly foolish.
But one little mouse was not so foolish.
Her name was Mabela, and her father had taught her cleverness.
Her father always told her,
"Mabela, when you are out and about, keep your ears open and LISTEN.
　　Mabela, when you are out and about, keep your eyes open and LOOK AROUND YOU.
　　Mabela, when you speak, pay attention to what you are SAYING.
　　Mabela, if you have to move, MOVE FAST."
Good advice for a mouse!

One day the Cat came to the mouse village.
"Dear Mice, I come to offer you a special invitation.
It has been decided that you may join the secret CAT CLUB."
The mice were SO excited. "We get to join the CAT CLUB!"
"We get to join the CAT CLUB!"
"Yes, my dears. Come to my house on Monday morning and I will teach you all the secrets of the CAT."

Monday morning bright and early, all the little mice were there.
"Oh my, you have ALL arrived! How delicious—I mean, How *delightful*."
"Now you must learn the secret Cat Club song.
The song goes like this:

"When we are marching,
We NEVER look back.
The Cat is at the end—*Fo Feng*!
FO FENG!"

The mice all shouted loudly on the last "FO FENG!"

"Now line up in a straight line."
Mabela got to march in front, because she was the smallest of them all.

And at the end came—the CAT!

"Now march into the forest" called the Cat. "And remember—never ever look back!"

Off they marched. Mabela was leading the way so proudly.

"When we are marching,
We NEVER look back.
The Cat is at the end—*Fo Feng*!
FO FENG!"

Every time the mice shouted *"Fo Feng!"* the Cat would *"Fo Feng"* the last mouse in line.

[Make a grabbing motion with your hand (paw) when you shout "Fo Feng!" and then let out a little "eek."]

Mabela was marching happily along.
"When we are marching,
We NEVER look back.
The Cat is at the end—*Fo Feng*!
FO FENG!"

[Repeat this several times. You can let out a little "eek" every time the cat Fo Feng's another mouse.]
Suddenly Mabela remembered something her father had told her,
"Mabela, when you are out and about
Keep your ears open and LISTEN!"
She was not listening at all. Mabela stopped singing for a moment and listened.

She did not hear a long line of mice singing behind her. She heard a FEW mice.
And the Cat's voice was very close!

Then Mabela remembered something else her father had taught her,
  "Mabela, when you are out and about
  Keep your eyes open and LOOK AROUND YOU."
Mabela turned her head just a little to the left. Just a little to the right.
She did NOT see a long line of mice.
She saw a SHORT line of mice and the CAT was VERY CLOSE!

Then she remembered what else her father had said.
  "Mabela, when you speak,
  Pay attention to what you are SAYING!"
She listened to the words of her song.
  "When we are marching
  We NEVER look back.
  The Cat is at the end—*Fo Feng!*
  FO FENG!"

"The cat is at the end? What does THAT mean? No one is watching the CAT!"
Mabela turned right around. There was the Cat!
She had just FO FENGED the mouse behind Mabela!

Now Mabela remembered the LAST thing her father had taught her.
  "Mabela, if you have to move, MOVE FAST!"
Mabela DOVE into the bushes…so fast…so fast…
That the Cat pounced on nothing but—thorns! "OUCH!"
So the cat was stuck and Mabela escaped.
Mabela lived to tell this story.
She told it to her children…and to her children's children.
Limba parents are STILL telling this story to their children.
It is good to remember the things Mabela's father taught her.
  When you are out and about, keep your ears open and LISTEN.
  "When you are out and about, keep your eyes open and LOOK AROUND YOU!
  When you speak, pay attention to what you are SAYING.
  And, if you ever have to move—MOVE FAST!"

Limba grandparents say, "If a person is clever, it is because someone has taught them their cleverness." So if your parents or your teacher try to teach you some cleverness, keep your ears open and LISTEN!

Mabela the Clever

Piano

When we are | marching we | never look | back. The | cat is at the | end. Fo | Feng! FO | FENG!

Source: You can find a beautifully illustrated picture book version of this story in *Mabela the Clever* by Margaret Read MacDonald, illustrated by Tim Coffey (Chicago: Albert Whitman, 2001). The story was retold from Ruth Finnegan's *Limba Stories and Storytelling* (Oxford: Oxford University Press, 1967). Dr. Finnegan collected the tale in 1964 from Kirinkoma Konteh, a young man of Kamabai, Sierra Leone.

About Telling the Story

In the picture book version the cat stuffs the caught mice into a bag and the mice escape at the end. In the folktale, as told by the Limba people, the cat actually eats the mice. You can decide how you want to tell the story.

Extending the Tale

- Retell the story and let the children act it out. Choose a Mabela, a cat, everyone else is a mouse. It is helpful to have an adult in the room to take the part of the cat. You may also need help making sure the mice sit back down after they are caught. Begin the tale with "Once a cat came to the Mouse Country." The cat enters and the mice gather around. Tell the dialog between the cat and the mouse. Older children will be able to repeat their lines after you. Line the mice up behind Mabela with the cat at the rear and lead them around the room as you sing. Every time the mice shout "Fo Feng!" the cat should grab the last mouse. The mouse then goes and sits back down.

Have the mice call "Eek!" when they are caught. At the end, the cat dives into the bushes and is stuck as Mabela escapes.

- Stick puppet figures for this tale can be found at www.margaretreadmacdonald.com. Click on "Books," type "Mabela the Clever," scroll to "Activities." A reader's theater for *Mabela the Clever* is also found there.

- View *Mabela the Clever:* DVD (Nutmeg Media, 2007), with story told by author.

- See Birte Harksen playing "Mabela the Clever" with her Icelandic pre-schoolers at www.youtube.com/watch?v=a3qK86zJgs.

- Make a class book of cleverness. What wisdom can we share with each other? You can use the sentence starter, "Remember, when you're out and about _____!"

Not Our Problem
A Folktale from Burma

A King sat with his Advisor eating honey on puffed rice.
A drop of honey fell from the King's mouth onto the windowsill.
"Your Majesty!" said his Advisor, "A drop of honey has fallen onto the windowsill."

"Never mind," said the King. "It is not our problem."

The drop of honey dripped down the windowsill and fell to the ground below the palace.
A fly lit on the drop of honey and began to eat it.
But a gecko jumped on the fly and began to eat IT.

"Your Majesty, a fly was eating the honey that fell from your mouth.
And now a gecko is eating the fly that was eating the honey."

Never mind," said the King. "It is not our problem."

A cat *pounced* on the gecko and began to eat it up.
A DOG ran out from under the palace and attacked the CAT.
Now the dog and the cat were fighting under the palace.

"Your Majesty a cat was eating the gecko and a DOG has attacked the cat.

They are fighting under the palace."

"Never mind," said the King. "It is not our problem."

The owner of the cat saw the dog attacking her cat.
She ran out with a broom and began to beat the dog.
But when the owner of the dog saw the woman beating his dog,
He ran out and began to beat *her.*
"Your Majesty, that drop of honey that fell from your mouth...a fly tried to eat it and a gecko ate the fly and a cat ate the gecko and a dog attacked the cat and now the owner of the cat has attacked the dog and the owner of the dog has attacked the woman who attacked his dog and two people are now fighting under the palace. I should send someone to stop the fight."

"Never mind," sighed the king. "It is not our problem."

Soon the friends of the woman saw her being attacked. They hurried to defend her.
But the friends of the man saw *him* being attacked. They rushed to defend him.
A large fistfight broke out under the palace.

"Your Majesty," pleaded the Advisor, "Now the woman's friends have attacked the man and his friends have attacked her friends. There is a great fight going on right under the palace. We should do something to stop this."

"Never mind," insisted the king. "It is not our problem."
Soldiers were passing through town just then.
When they saw the fight, they rushed to break it up.
But when they heard the situation, some sided with the man,
And some sided with the woman.
The soldiers began to argue among themselves.
In the argument a gun was pulled out and...fired!
And a civil war broke out!

In the fighting, the palace was burned to the ground.
The King and his Advisor stood in the ashes.
"I think," said the King, "The drop of honey *was* our problem."

Source: *Peace Tales: World Folktales to Talk About* by Margaret Read MacDonald (Atlanta: August House, 1992), p. 18-21. Other versions of this tale appear in: *A Kingdom for a Drop of Honey* by Maung Htin Aung and Helen G. Trager (New York: Parent's Magazine Press, 1969) and *Tales from Thailand* by Marian Davies Toth (Rutland, Vt.: Charles Tuttle, 1971). *This is Motif N381 Drop of honey causes chain of accidents.*

Extending the Tale

- Research Burma/Myanmar, the country from which this tale came.

- Share other chain tales, such as *Why Mosquitoes Buzz in People's Ears* by Verna Aardema, illustrated by Leo and Diane Dillon (Dial, 1975), or *The Old Woman and Her Pig* by Margaret Read MacDonald (Harper Collins, 2007). Discuss cause and effect.

- Write your own chain story of actions that lead one to another. You could even create a chain story set in your own school.

- Compare this story with the British saying: "For want of a nail the shoe was lost. For want of a shoe, the horse was lost. For want of a horse the rider was lost. For want of a rider, the battle was lost. For want of a battle the war was lost. All for the want of a horseshoe nail." This adage dates back to the 15th century and may have historical connections with Richard III.

- For older students: Study other wars. What series of events led to them?

Ready...Set...Tell!

Select a story from this book or a favorite you've heard before that you would like to refer back to during the school year. Think about how you could use this tale in the first week of school. What would be a way to play with story more than once, so that students embed the message? Make a plan to share three stories during the first week of school next year. Remember, you don't need to tell these stories only once. Re-visit them throughout the year. Your students will be thrilled when you do!

Chapter 2: CHARACTER—
Forming Character Through Storytelling

In each telling the story itself changes a little, changes direction, and that in turn changes you and me. So be very careful not only how you repeat it, but in how you remember it…More often than you realize it, the world is shaped by two things…stories told and the memories they leave behind.

—Vera Nazarian, *Dreams of the Compass Rose*

People have always used stories to convey important messages about how to behave within society. "Stay on the path, Little Red!" "Don't judge a book by its cover, Beauty!" We all recognize these messages instantly. Stories are a perfect vehicle for sharing common values. While we relax and enjoy listening to a good story, the underlying messages enter our hearts and stay nestled in our minds. There are countless stories that you can draw upon to focus students on messages that they *need* to hear at any given moment.

As children enter the world of story, they identify easily with the tale's main characters. Following them through their trials, the child discovers ways to overcome obstacles, ways to react kindly to those met along the way. Folktales often highlight the rewards of virtuous actions and the consequences of treating others poorly. By selecting stories carefully, we can help children experience situations vicariously that will guide their actions in the future.

Throughout the ages, stories have been told as a way to set up guidelines for appropriate behavior for children and adults alike. Because stories are told about anonymous characters, they are a way to "say without saying." The Liberian teller Won-Ldy Paye notes that in his Dan culture, if the chief was misbehaving, no one would dare say a word to him directly. But the storyteller could construct a tale about Spider doing exactly what the chief was up to and getting his comeuppance. Everyone would know whom the storyteller was really talking about. Tales can be used the same way in our classrooms. Without singling out the child who is acting inappropriately, a tale can be told of a character who behaves in this way—everyone gets the message.

When we have students who are not participating 100 percent in group work, we take a break and share "Koala and Tree Kangaroo" (found at the end of this chapter), a story of two friends who try to dig a well together. Tree Kangaroo works hard, while Koala naps. Students instantly recognize themselves in the story. "Are you a Koala or a Tree Kangaroo?" How would you feel if you were in that situation?" "What would you do?" Stories can offer a moment of reflection for us to think about our own actions and how they affect others.

The fifth grade class I taught was having a hard time seeing each other's point of view. I immediately thought of the "Blind Man and the Elephant" story. [Five blind men each touch a different part of the elephant and deduce that it is like a fan, a hose, etc.] They listened as I described each part, then left the ending without stating the moral. One outspoken student stood up and said, "Well, why didn't they just talk about it! They could speak, couldn't they?" The room was SILENT. I let them sit in silence for about five minutes. This is very unusual for a fifth-grade class. Then they left for lunch. After lunch was done the students in conflict came to me and told me how they had worked out their differences. Oh, the power of a few words, spoken at the right time!

—Jan Morgan, Grade 5, Bremerton, WA

Story as an Emotional Guide for Children

Stories offer an important guide for how to act, and they also help students develop emotionally. Psychologists have found story useful in helping children work through their own problems and in giving them a story structure through which to interpret the events of their lives. In *The Uses of Enchantment: The Meaning and Importance of Fairy Tales*, Bruno Bettelheim makes a strong argument that scary stories function with great importance in the imaginative life of the child. The story framework allows children to experience raw emotion in bite-sized pieces that they are able to digest easily. They are safe in the context of the story and can play with rage, with terror, with disgust in a way that is not acceptable outside the realm of story. In recent years, we have greatly sanitized our folktales so that little of this raw emotion remains, but our students still need it.

We know a talented Brazilian storyteller, Roberto Carlos Ramos, who is renowned for his "jump" tales. In one quiet ghost story, he will make the audience leap out of their skins ten times. Roberto Carlos says that, in his cultural tradition, these jump tales are critical for children to mature. Every time you JUMP, you grow just a little bit more.

Stories can help students connect with difficult emotions that may be hard to grapple with in ordinary life. In the same way, story helps children explore and strengthen those positive qualities we hope to develop in our students such as displaying empathy for others, showing commitment to a task, asking important questions. Through listening to stories, our students envision ways to live happily and successfully in our world.

Developing Character Through Story

A carefully placed tale can help your students reflect on their own behaviors. Look for stories that focus on the needs of your class at this moment in time. As we have already mentioned, once a story is shared with the entire class, it can be referred back to throughout the year as a quick reminder about classroom expectations.

Here are a few examples of how teachers have used the stories in this book to focus on character development:

Accepting the differences of others: In "How to Break a Bad Habit" (p. 143) Monkey and Rabbit intolerantly accuse each other of having bad habits.

> *I told this one in response to a student who is always "telling on" the boy next to him who chews on his shirt, which I admit is gross, but something we can all choose to ignore. I told this story, and followed it with a discussion about bad habits. We included discussion of habits of others which we could kindly choose to ignore, and those we should personally work on breaking.*
>
> —Kerith Telestai, Grade 5, Sienna Elementary, Boise, ID.

> *I told "How to Break a Bad Habit" to the guitar class. It was fitting because these students needed a lesson about sharing and appreciating each other's differences. The story was short and appropriate for this age level. Some of the students even commented on the relevance of the story for all high school students. One girl said, "I wish more teachers would tell relevant stories that applied to us high school students."*
>
> —Ryan Lewis, Music Instructor, Cedarcrest High School, Duvall, WA.

Accepting Responsibility: "Not Our Problem" (p. 29) shows a king who refuses to take responsibility for a spilled drop of honey. The results are disastrous.

> *I told "Not Our Problem" today because I was so tired of students telling me that they didn't make the mess in the classroom. Then I asked them to clean up to go home. It worked! They were willing to clean up and jokingly kept saying, "Not my problem."*
>
> — Kelly Kennedy, Grade 3-4, Adams Elementary, Seattle, WA.

Focusing on Character Traits in the School

Many schools implement some kind of school-wide focus on character traits throughout the year. As the school's resident storyteller, you might offer to share tales linked to the character traits your school is highlighting at assemblies. Here is a quick guide to stories in this book that focus on commonly used character traits:

Trustworthiness: Share the story of "Koala and Tree Kangaroo." Koala was not a trustworthy friend.

Respect: In the tale "How to Break a Bad Habit," Monkey and Rabbit decide to give each other respect, despite their bad habits. In "Grandfather Bear is Hungry," Chipmunk is given five stripes as a sign of respect for his actions. "Little Basket Weaver" earns respect for her hard work. Ms. Mouse in "Ms. Mouse Needs a Friend" shows lack of respect for her friends.

Responsibility: In "Old Man Wombat" Mother Kangaroo shows great responsibility in looking after her little Joey, as well as Old Man Wombat. The King in "Not Our Problem" does *not* assume responsibility, with dire results. "Monkeys in the Rain" do not take responsibility for their future.

Fairness: There is not a fair division of labor in the story of "Koala and Tree Kangaroo."

Caring: "Grandfather Bear is Hungry," "Old Man Wombat," and "Little Basket Weaver" all feature caring characters. In "Frog and Locust" both characters care about the environment. "The Elephants and the Bees" take care of each other. And the grandmother in "Squeaky Door" certainly cares about her little grandson.

Citizenship: Frog and Locust are good citizens as they work together to bring rain. The King in "Not Our Problem" is *not* a good citizen.

Cooperation: The goats in "Two Goats on a Bridge" learn to cooperate. "Frog and Locust Bring the Rain" shows cooperation to achieve an end. In "Lifting the Sky" an entire community must learn to work together.

Tolerance: In "How to Break a Bad Habit," Monkey and Rabbit learn to accept each other's habit. "Little Basket Weaver" suggests to the listener that we should be understanding of different learners. "Ms. Mouse Needs a Friend" is an example of intolerance.

Independence: "Mabela the Clever" takes on a leadership role in an emergency.

Commitment: "Little Basket Weaver" commits to her task. In "Koala and Tree Kangaroo," Tree Kangaroo commits to his task, but Koala does not.

Stories to Take You Further

Here are a few collections with more stories to help you think about moral issues.

MacDonald, Margaret Read. *Peace Tales: World Folktales to Talk About*. Atlanta: August House, 1995. Pathways to war and pathways to peace are the topics of these tales.

Norfolk, Bobby and Sherry. *The Moral of the Story: Folktales for Character Development*. Little Rock: August House, 1999. Twelve tales, with notes on use are accompanied by a discussion of use of storytelling for character education.

Pearmain, Elisa Davy. *Doorways to the Soul: 52 Wisdom Tales from Around the World*. Cleveland, OH: Pilgrim Press, 1998. Short moral tales, easy-to-tell.

_____. *Once Upon a Time: Storytelling to Teach Character and Prevent Bullying. Lessons from 99 Multicultural Folk Tales for Grades K-8*. Character Development Group, 2006. All 99 tales deal with various character traits and include follow-up activities. Also has information on how to learn and tell stories.

Let's Look at Grandfather Bear

Consider ways you might link Grandfather Bear to character education. Little Chipmunk demonstrates caring for others by sharing his food. He and Grandfather Bear discuss the problem and solve it together, which models successful conflict resolution. Grandfather Bear returns chipmunk's kindness by giving chipmunk a mark of honor.

Try a Tale!

Two of our favorite tales to use for character development are "Koala and Tree Kangaroo" and "Ms. Mouse Needs a Friend." Children really get excited about Koala's bad behavior and are ready to discuss this after the story. "Ms. Mouse Needs a Friend" shows the folly of disrespecting one's friends and has many clear classroom applications.

Koala and Tree Kangaroo
An Aboriginal Folktale from Australia

One year there was no rain.
The pools dried up.
The streams dried up.
The animals were dying of thirst.

Tree Kangaroo said to his best friend, Koala,
"When I was little there was a time like this.
My mother took me in her pouch and traveled.
We went over a mountain and down a valley…
Over a mountain and down a valley…
We came to a dry stream bed.
My mother dug and dug and she found water.
She had a sip and I had a sip.
And we survived.

"Could you find that place again?" asked Koala.
"I don't know. I could try."

"Then let's travel!"

They went over a mountain and down a valley. *[Lead the audience in hand gestures]*
Over a mountain and down a valley.
They came to a dry stream bed.
"Is this the place?" asked Koala.
Tree Kangaroo looked all around. "I don't think so."

"Then let's travel!"

They went over a mountain and down a valley.
Over a mountain and down a valley.
They came to a dry stream bed.
"Is this the place?" asked Koala.
"I don't think so."

"Then let's travel!"

Over a mountain and down a valley.
Over a mountain and down a valley.
Another dry stream bed.
"Is this the place?"
Tree Kangaroo looked all around.
"It looks right. I think this is the place."

"Then let's dig!" said Koala. "You can dig first. You found the place."
Koala sat down in the shade.
And Tree Kangaroo began to dig.

He dug and he dug and he threw out the dirt. *[Lead audience in digging]*
He dug and he dug and he threw out the dirt.
He dug and he dug and he got soooo tired. *[wipe brow]*

"Okay, Koala. It's your turn to dig now."
"I'm coming," said Koala. "Just a minute."

Koala took two steps. "OOOOHHHH! I stepped on a thorn!
I've got a thorn in my paw! I can't dig yet."

Koala sat back down in the shade.
Tree Kangaroo dug.

He dug and he dug and he threw out the dirt.
He dug and he dug and he threw out the dirt.
He dug and he dug and he got soooo tired.

Okay, Koala. It's your turn.
I'm really getting tired now. You come dig for a while."

"I'm coming. I want to help." Koala took two steps.
"OOOOHHHH! I've got a cramp; in my TAIL.
In those days Koala had a long bushy tail. [Stress this point]
I can't dig yet. You go ahead."

Koala sat back down in the shade.
Tree Kangaroo kept on digging.

He dug and he dug and he threw out the dirt.
He dug and he dug and he threw out the dirt.
He dug and he dug and he got soooo tired.
"Come on, Koala. I've had three turns.
YOU take a turn now."

Then Tree Kangaroo saw something in the bottom of the hole.
"I think I see something damp. We might be close to water."

"Oh, *you* go ahead, Tree Kangaroo. You've done all that digging.
You might as well have the fun of finding the water."

And Koala kept sitting in the shade.
So Tree Kangaroo kept on digging.

He dug and he dug and he threw out the dirt.
He dug and he dug and he threw out the dirt.
He dug and he dug and he got soooo tired.

"Koala, come on…OH! I think I see it!
The water is *coming*!"

Koala jumped up.
He RAN down to the hole.
He PUSHED Tree Kangaroo out of the way.
He stuck his head right down in that hole and started slurping water.

Koala's long, bushy tail was sticking up out of the hole waving in Tree Kangaroo's face.
Tree Kangaroo looked at that tail swishing back and forth.
Tree Kangaroo just reached out and SNATCHED that tail off!
Koala backed out of the hole.
He looked at Tree Kangaroo.
He didn't say a thing.

He knew he had been lazy.

He knew he had not done his part.

He knew he had not been a good friend.

If you see Koala in the zoo,

Take a look at his tail.

He has hardly any tail at all!

When you see that remember:

It is important to always do your part

And be a good friend.

Source: "Why Koala Has No Tail" in *Look Back and See: Twenty Lively Tales for Gentle Tellers* by Margaret Read MacDonald (New York: H.W. Wilson, 1991), retold from "Why Koala Has No Tail" in *Aboriginal Legends: Animal Tales* by A.W. Reed (French Forest, Australia: Reed Books Pty. Ltd., 1978). The specific group from which this story comes was not given. Motif A2233.1.1 *Animals refuse to help dig well: may not drink from river or spring.*

Extending the Tale

- Locate Australia on a map.

- Learn about Australian Aboriginal groups. Learn about koalas and tree kangaroos. Find a picture of a tree kangaroo and discuss how they are similar to and different than other kangaroos.

- Working in teams, act this story out as tandem telling.

- You can also find lesson plans for using *Why Koala Has a Stumpy Tail* by Martha Hamilton and Mitch Wiess at www.storycove.com. Select "Animations and Lesson Plans" then click on "Lesson Plans" next click on "Why Koala Has a Stumpy Tail" and select "Activities."

Ms. Mouse Needs a Friend
A Chucha Folktale from Siberia

One cold winter morning Ms. Mouse woke up feeling thirsty.
She took her little cup and her little hatchet and went to the frozen pond.
Ms. Mouse sat down and chopped a hole in the ice.
Then she dipped her cup in the cool water and began to drink.
"Aaahhh…" How good that cold water tasted!

Ms. Mouse drank it all down.
She dipped her little cup and had another cool drink. "Aaahhh…"
Just one more. "Aaahhh…"
Ms. Mouse dipped her cup and drank again. "Aaahhh…"

Ms. Mouse packed away her cup and started to stand up.
But… "Oh! Oh!"
Ms. Mouse had sat on the ice so long her TAIL had frozen fast to the ice!

"Eee! Eee! I'm STUCK! Eee! Eee! I'm STUCK!" She began to wail.

Then Ms. Mouse thought, "I must find a friend to rescue me.
Who could I call on for help?"
She remembered Snowshoe Rabbit.
Ms. Mouse began to call,
"Snowshoe Rabbit! Help, Help! Snowshoe Rabbit! Help, Help!
I need a friend!"

Snowshoe Rabbit heard her. He came out of his hole.
"I'm coming, Ms. Mouse! I'll be your friend."
Snowshoe Rabbit came running down the hill on his big snowshoe feet.

But when she saw him coming, Ms. Mouse began to snicker.
"Oh, look at those silly big feet. What stupid big feet Snowshoe Rabbit has!"

When Snowshoe Rabbit heard her, he stopped. His feelings were hurt.
"I guess she doesn't want me for a friend after all."
Snowshoe Rabbit turned around and went back to his hole.

"Oh. Oh," said Ms. Mouse. "I think I said the wrong thing.

Now who can I call? Maybe Mink could help me.
Mink! Help, Help! Mink! Help, Help! I need a friend!"

Mink heard Ms. Mouse calling. He came out of his den.
"I'm coming, Ms. Mouse. I'll be your friend."

Mink came sliding down the path to the pond.
He put out his paw to help Ms. Mouse and hollered, "I'll be your friend!"

But Ms. Mouse began to sneer.
"Yuck! Yuck! What BAD BREATH you have! ICK! What BAD BREATH!"

Mink was offended. "Maybe she doesn't want me for a friend after all."
Mink turned away and scurried back to his den.

"Oh. Oh," said Ms. Mouse. "I think I said the wrong thing."

"Now who can I call? Fox! He might help.
Fox! Help, help! Fox! Help, help! I need a friend!"

Fox, sleeping in his den, heard her.
"I'm coming, Ms. Mouse. I'll be your friend."
Fox came running down the snowy hill waving his long red tail.

But before he could put out his paw to aid her, Ms. Mouse began to snicker.
"Just look at that long stupid TAIL! What an ugly tail!"

Fox felt very bad. "Maybe she doesn't want me for a friend after all."
Fox turned and hurried back to his home.

"Oh. Oh," said Ms. Mouse. "I think I said the wrong thing."

Who can I call? BEAR! BEAR! Help, help!
BEAR! Help, help! I need a friend!"

Bear was sleeping in his den. He heard that mouse calling and calling.
"I'm coming, Ms. Mouse! I'll be your friend!"

Bear came so fast right down to the pond. "Here I COME!"
"WHACK!" With one stroke of his huge paw he knocked Ms. Mouse free.

"There you are, Ms. Mouse! No need to thank me."
And he was gone back up the hill and into his den before she could say one thing.

Ms. Mouse was free.
But that huge bear had hit her so hard that it broke her little tail right off.
Poor Ms. Mouse. She ran off home crying, "Eee! Eee! I chose the wrong friend. Eee! Eee! I chose the wrong friend."

Don't be like Ms. Mouse. If someone offers you a hand in friendship—take it.
Just overlook their faults and be a friend.
Or you might end up like Ms. Mouse—with a strong friend, but NO tail!

Source: *A Parent's Guide to Storytelling by Margaret Read MacDonald* (Little Rock: August House Publishers, 2001), p. 42-27. The story was retold from *Animal Stories from the Far North: Kutkha the Raven*. Trans. By Fainna Solasko, illustrated by Y. Rachov (Moscow: Malysh Publishers, 1981).

About Telling the Story

You might let the children pretend to dip a cup in the pond and sip water with you. Encourage them to call for help with Ms. Mouse.

Extending the Tale

- Expand the story by adding more animals. What animals live in Siberia? What fault might Ms. Mouse find with those animals if they tried to help her? The story has a set pattern. You can retell the story and add in other characters.

- Assign roles and act out the story.

- Find Siberia on a map and learn about the climate and environment there.

- Talk about what one needs to do to be a good friend.

Ready…Set…Tell!

How does your school approach character education? Think about the words that are used in your school community to help students focus on developing character. Honesty? Empathy? Commitment? Select one and then choose a story from this book or another source that would help you spark a discussion with your class. Share it this week! Then, take the time to have a genuine discussion with your students about how they connect with the characters in the story and what meaning the tale has for them in their own lives. The results may surprise you!

Chapter 3: COMMUNICATION—
Using Story to Develop
Language and Literacy Skills

Whenever I'm asked what advice I have for young writers, I always say that the first thing is to read, and to read a lot. The second thing is to write. And the third thing, which I think is absolutely vital, is to tell stories and listen closely to the stories you're being told.

— John Green

We are entrusted with a monumental task in our work with students in schools. In the few years children spend with us, we need to take them from pre-literacy to mastery of language and communication. We need to shape literate citizens who are capable of listening, reading, and viewing critically and who are equally able to communicate and create through writing, speaking, and performing. Not a small task! Of course, this means different things at different stages—learning the alphabet, revising a story, writing with voice, speaking clearly, adding detail, using imagery, speaking with expression, and making connections, to name a few.

Fortunately, storytelling is a key that can help unlock the doors of language and literacy for all of our students. In this chapter, we'll look at how you can use storytelling to help children express themselves orally and in writing. We'll also examine how storytelling helps students become better readers and listeners.

Story Grammar

Just as our sentences are organized by the rules of grammar, our stories have a grammar all their own. Educational researchers talk about "story grammar" and its importance in literacy development. James B. Byrnes and Barbara A. Wasik in *Language and Literacy Development: What Educators Need to Know* (NY: Guilford Press, 2009) remind us that children develop their own understanding of story over time and through exposure to different types of narratives. Developing this internal framework for the "rules" of story is an important part of becoming literate. The idea that a story will have a setting and that the main character will face a challenge are parts of story grammar. As we listen to more and more stories, we create a set of story "schemata" in our minds. We anticipate what will come next based on the scaffolding we have developed by listening to stories in the past. Students who have created a strong set of internal story schemata are able to make better predictions and better inferences while they are reading and they are able to develop narratives with greater ease when writing.

Repeated exposure to narrative in different shapes over time helps students internalize this story grammar. Every time you tell a story in your classroom, your students are developing their own story schemata and deepening their understanding of what makes a story. This is the rich soil in which our learners can blossom as readers and writers, and we begin tending this garden with our very youngest students.

Emergent Literacy

Storytelling is a wonderful way to welcome young children to the exciting world of language. Playing with story in early childhood classrooms provides a warm and engaging way for children to experience language in a joyful context. When telling to these youngest listeners, we look for stories that let us play with language. The refrain in "Teeny Weeny Bop," found at the end of this chapter, is lively and rhythmic. "To Market to Market, to buy a fat pig, home again, home again, jiggity-jig!" When we play with the story in repeated telling, we ask students to make up new rhymes as they go to market. Stories with predictable patterns, like "Teeny Weeny Bop," "The Squeaky Door," and many others in this book, are perfect for helping the youngest learners internalize story structure and eventually retell stories on their own.

Once young learners have heard a story, they are often eager to take on the characters themselves and act it out. If you work with young children, try to make space for this in your day. Acting out the story helps children internalize the narrative structure and solidify those story schemata that are so important for developing confident readers and writers. It also allows children to engage with the vocabulary and unique language of the story in their own playful way. We've heard wonderful conversations between students as they help each other sequence the story and work together to embellish the story in new and unexpected ways. All the folktales in this book lend themselves well to acting out and we encourage you to try bringing a story to life through dramatic play—whatever the age of your students!

In early childhood settings, we like to revisit stories as many times and in as many different ways as possible. After we've acted out the story as a class and students are comfortable with the story, we often encourage students to retell the story with friends during choice time in a storytelling center. You could have name tags available for each character, i.e., Teeny Weeny Bop, Pig, Pet Seller. You could have just a few props that are important to the story, such as a basket or a coin. Of course, there are myriad ways to engage with the story again—puppets, felt boards, story boards—and all of those learning activities that early childhood teachers incorporate so well into their daily instruction can be modified to welcome a new folktale.

We find that stories in the early years often spill out of the classroom and onto the playground, too! We'll see students playing "Mabela the Clever" and marching around—who will be the cat this time? Sometimes, we'll find a couple of students quietly acting out Grandfather Bear—"You be chipmunk first and then it's my turn!" Playing with story in this way is important language work for our youngest learners.

So, storytelling in the early grades lays the groundwork for our students to become confident language users. Let's look now at how storytelling can help students develop their writing and reading skills as they get older.

Writing

Students exposed to beautiful oral language are more likely to use interesting language in their own writing. Studies have indicated that children who are exposed to storytelling have an increased use and understanding of narrative structures (Gebracht 1984, Whitman 2006, and others). When your students listen to a variety of tales and a variety of tellers, they will acquire a stronger sense of language that they can then pour into their own work.

Any time you share a new story, there are countless ways you could follow it up with a writing activity. Write a reflection on the story. Write a new ending to the story. Retell the story from the point of view of one of the characters. Whatever your writing focus is, you can demonstrate through a told story.

Storytelling as a Part of the Writing Process

The craft of writing is complicated and requires students to tap into a wide range of skills as they work. We all have students who struggle with the composition of their pieces because the mechanics of writing get in the way. Storytelling can help. When students are working on writing narrative texts, we have found great success inserting storytelling into the writing process. We have our students tell their story before they even begin to write. The act of telling the story orally sharpens the focus of the tale before the actual task of writing begins. When students are comfortable telling stories, they are able to use this skill to support their own creative writing.

Nat focused his Masters of Education research on the effect of inserting storytelling into the prewriting and editing process with second-grade students writing narratives. This small-scale study has potentially big implications for the way we teach writing. When students were asked to "tell" their story to a peer, they showed more sophisticated sentence structure, a higher degree of organization, and stronger word choice in their final, written work.

Lucy Calkins and other writing specialists call this "rehearsing" a story. These rehearsals are critical for students to develop their own voices. Allowing your students to voice their story multiple times, to several different buddies, will help them improve their tale even more. Once the story is shaped in the mind through repeated telling, it is much easier to set it to paper. The listening partner can offer helpful suggestions to the teller: What was unclear? What was especially interesting? What else would they like to know about the story? Whatever method you use in your classroom for students to give constructive peer feedback for writing will apply just as easily in the context of a told story. We have had success using the popular "two stars and a wish." The listener responds with two positive comments and a question e.g., "I really thought this part was interesting because _____." I thought this part of the story was exciting because _____." I wonder if you could make this part more clear if you were to add _____?"

Kieran Egan in his seminal work *An Imaginative Approach to Teaching* (Jossey-Bass 2005) suggests that we all have a deep sense of narrative shaped by the stories told to us and by us. A lifetime of stored narrative structure, cultural reality, and emotion are tapped when students tell their story orally in the writing process.

Thinking of the Audience

Telling a story also requires you to think about your audience carefully. This is important training for writers. We tell our students to consider their audience and make sure they are writing for that particular audience. The perfect way to practice this skill is to tell stories orally to an actual audience who can give immediate feedback. This technique helps place our audience directly at the center of our storytelling when we're writing.

Developing Voice Through Personal Narratives

We want to give our students ample opportunities to tell their own stories in their own voice. We believe that the heart of all teaching is asking our students, "What is *your story?*" We need to give our students the time to explore this and to let them know that we honor their stories, their voices. Who am I? What is important to me and why? These are questions that students can explore through their writing and their own personal storytelling.

In order for students to do this, of course, they need modeling and instruction. Just as reading a wide range of authors helps children develop an understanding for individual author voice in writing, listening to a selection of different storytellers can help our students develop their own voice. And whose voice do they need to hear the most? *Yours!* It's important to share your own stories with your students. From the little stories about small moments in your life to the big stories you remember from your childhood…about a time when you learned an important lesson that has stayed with you for life. Big stories or small ones, your students deserve to hear your stories. They are asking the same questions of you as their teacher that you are asking of them—who are *you*? What is *your* story? We find that the minute we begin to share a personal anecdote, no matter how insignificant, every eye in the room is focused and all ears are waiting to hear our story.

By sharing my own stories with the students and modeling a brainstorm of stories I would like to write or tell about, students became inspired to share theirs. The enthusiasm in the room was contagious. At our appointed story time after lunch today I was prepared to tell the story of my bike wreck on 72nd Street. The kids loved it because they could all relate to crashing their bikes! Every one of them wanted to tell me about their own bike wreck. I think I will take this story and create a writing prompt where they have to tell me their own stories on paper. What a great connection to another academic subject. I didn't expect to end up with this little gem! An observation I have about telling personal stories: I didn't feel as worried about leaving out details from these stories. I had lived them and knew them by heart!

— Sandy Anthony, Fairmount Elementary, Mukilteo, WA

Folklore Genres

Telling stories helps students develop their own voice as an author and clarify *what* it is they would like to say. Storytelling can also offer ideas for *how* your students can express themselves in writing. Students who have heard a rich and varied assortment of folktales over the years have a stronger sense of how to develop their own stories.

A folktale is a story that has been passed from person to person. It has been shaped through repeated telling among the folk and exists in many variants. Listening to folktales exposes students to a wide range of narrative genres that are available to them as authors. Note that the many folktale genres we list are sub-categories of the "folktale." In other words a "fairy tale" is just one kind of "folktale."

- Animal Tales

- Circular Stories and Chain Stories (stick beats dog, dog bites pig, pig jumps over stile)

- Epics (tale cycles of one hero, i.e., King Arthur, Roland, Shaka)

- Fables (short tales of animals or humans with a moral)

- Fairytales (folktales with magical elements)

- Humorous Anecdotes and Jokes

- Legends (historical, religious, legends of place)

- Myths (tales of gods, the belief tales of a culture)

- Riddle Tales

- Pourquoi Stories (How and Why Stories)

- Tall Tales

- Trickster Tales

- Urban Legends

- Wisdom Tales

Once you've shared a variety of folktale genres with your students, these same tales can provide excellent scaffolding for creative writing. Playing with folktales has always been a favorite avenue for creating writing prompts in the classroom. Note that your students are not writing 'folktales'. They are writing stories based on a folktale model. By definition a folktale must have been passed down from person to person and has no author.

Here are a few ideas to get you started:

- Re-write "Little Red Riding Hood" from the perspective of the wolf.

- Write a new version of "The Gingerbread Man" set in your hometown.

- Write a Pourquoi tale, a how-and-why story, explaining "How the Tiger Got His Stripes."

The possibilities are endless, let your imagination and your curricular focus guide you.

Literary Devices

Sharing stories is also a good way to help students develop a sense of literary devices. Watch for tales that use alliteration, such as "Fo Feng!" shout the mice in "Mabela the Clever." This is not translatable as it is the Limba people's attempt to imitate the scratching sound of the cat. Notice the rhythm in Little Crab's chant, the rhyme in "Teeny Weeny Bop."

Watch for imagery, personification, simile, and metaphor. Point these figures of speech out as you share the stories. Hearing these devices repeatedly, and even telling the stories themselves, your students will develop a better feel for these literary devices. This will inform their work as writers.

While today's email, texting, and even conversation turns language into clipped phrases and emoticons, storytelling revives the immense power of language to capture location, emotion, and relationships. We owe it to children to share this linguistic heritage with them, to show them what language can do when used expertly…Good stories offer the best metaphors, the most mellifluous rhythms, and the most enticing adjectives to share the profound beauty of language.

— Brian Sturm, "The process of sharing stories with young people."
Knowledge Quest. Journal of the American Association of School Librarians, V. 36, No. 5. May/June 2008, p. 14.

Pocket Books

Our favorite "go-to" writing activity to follow-up any story is a 'Pocket Book'. We sometimes call it an "Abracadabra…POOF!" book when working with younger students. All you need is a piece of paper, a pair of scissors, and a little patience.

How to Make a Pocket Book

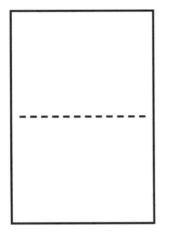

<<< 1. Fold a piece of paper in half the "hamburger" way.

2. Unfold the paper, then fold it in half again the "hot dog" way. >>>

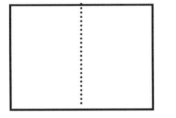

<<< 3. Unfold the paper, then fold it the hamburger way again.

4. Then fold it again the "mini-hamburger" way. >>>

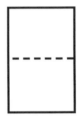

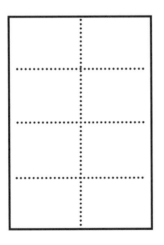

<<< 5. When you unfold it, your paper should look like this.

6. Fold it in half again the "hamburger" way with the fold at the top. >>>

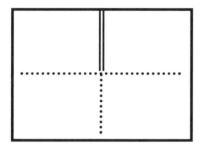

<<< 7. Take your sissors and cut down from the folded side to the intersection of the fold lines.

8. Unfold the paper and fold it again the "hotdog" way with the fold at the top. >>>

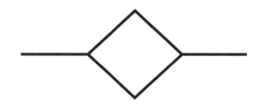

Now comes the tricky part.

<<< 9. Grab hold of each end and push the two sides together. The space in the middle will push open to make "fish lips."

10. Keep pushing until the paper ends up folded in a "+" then fold two adjacent sides around the others to form a four-page book. >>>

Abracadabra—POOF! Just like magic, you have a book ready to write in!

What we love about pocket books is that they provide exactly three pages, just enough for a quick notation about the beginning, middle, and end of a story. Younger students will often draw pictures and label them, while older students might write phrases or speech bubbles to help them remember the important details. Pocket stories are also fabulous because students can fit them in their pocket and then they are reminded of the story at home when they pull them out. The pocket story provides just enough information for the students to tell the story independently to mom or dad. Once your students begin making these, they'll have their pockets FULL of stories throughout the year!

Reading Comprehension

Storytelling not only helps students become more thoughtful writers, it also lets them develop critical reading skills. Important reading strategies, such as predicting and making connections, can be practiced through the context of storytelling without the pressure of decoding. Just as you would read a story and use "think-alouds" to help your students practice targeted skills, you can use a told story to practice important reading strategies with your students. Here are a few suggestions for how to apply storytelling to specific comprehension strategies.

Visualizing

One of the strategies we work hard to help readers develop is the ability to create images while reading. Storytelling is a natural way for students to practice making images. Encourage your students to share their images with each other. What do *you* think Little Crab saw under the sea? What do *you* think chipmunk's house was like? A natural extension to a storytelling session can be to have students paint or draw images that are inspired by the story. Have everyone illustrate one point from the story and see through a class mural how everyone builds characters and episodes differently in their own imaginations.

Summarizing

It is critical that we help children develop the ability to summarize what they have read succinctly. Any story map or other graphic organizer that you use to help your students summarize what they have read could be used just as easily with a told story. Here is one of our favorite activities to help students focus on summarizing—making a retelling wall. After telling a story, we ask students to think back on the story and hold a picture in their mind of a part of the story that has a strong image for them. Next, we ask students to draw a quick sketch of this part of the story on a post-it note. Students then place their post-it on a story timeline on the wall. This gives us an instant visual reminder to help with the retelling of the story. Often, once everyone has posted their sticky note, most of the important events in the story are already represented. We have a discussion about sequencing and make sure all of the events are in order. Then, we ask students to make a quick sketch to fill in any important events that are missing. We can use this timeline to help summarize the story as a class or individually. The poster stays on our wall as a retelling poster and students can revisit the timeline to help them retell the story. In addition to helping students sequence the events in the story and summarize the main ideas clearly, this activity also gives us a way to talk about how people visualize the same parts of the story differently and opens an interesting discussion about why students chose to sketch particular parts of the story.

I have students draw pictures of the setting, characters, problem, and solution. I have four large pieces of labeled paper on the white board and they paste their corresponding pictures to it. After we review the story elements on the posters, they write a summary. I explain that they just tell who was in the story, where it took place, what the problem was, and how it was solved. It was so easy after this activity. It took all the mystery and frustration out of summary writing.

— Tammie Enders, Grade 4, Glenwood Elementary, Seattle

In a similar technique, Daryl Buchman, of Kent, Washington uses story to teach sequencing to his fourth grade students. First he tells the story, emphasizing the transitional words. Then he tells the story again, asking the students to watch for the transitional words. Next he and the students together create a graphic organizer for the story on the board, writing down main events and transitional words. Now the students are ready to apply this same technique to the stories they are working on.

Predicting

Storytelling will activate your students' understanding of story schemata and enable them to make better predictions about what will happen next. The more they are exposed to narrative, the more sophisticated they can be in their thoughts about what might happen next while they are reading. We feel strongly that the majority of stories you tell should be told straight through for the sheer enjoyment of the tale, without stopping for teachable moments. When we are focusing on predicting as a reading strategy, however, we will choose a story or two that we use to pause throughout and ask students to "turn and talk" and share their predictions about what might happen next in the story. We then talk about how the predicting we have been doing with our partner while listening to the story is just like the predicting that you can be doing as a reader every time you *read* a story.

Inferring

Just as students will grow in their ability to make reasonable predictions while listening to tales, stories also help students develop their ability to "read between the lines." Listening and discussing stories helps children to think about motivation of characters. You can guide this development with thought-provoking questions: What is missing from the story? What information do we need to fill in ourselves? What do you think is the motivation for _____? Why do you think the king acted in that way? What would have happened if the princess didn't laugh? How do you think the bear felt at the end of the story?

Making Connections

Text to text, text to self, text to world—we work hard to develop readers who can make these connections. When you have a bank of shared stories that you have told to your class over the year, you have another common reference point that your students can connect to in their conversations about their reading. Students are quick to make connections between stories you tell, between stories and books you have read together, and to events that have happened in their own lives. We often find that our students make connections more quickly to stories we've told than to books we've read. Once you have a shared set of stories that your class has experienced together, you will be hearing "I have a connection to that story you told about…" often throughout the year.

Use the classic Venn Diagram to help students think about connections between stories by comparing and contrasting the elements of two similar tales. Choose two versions of one story and have your students analyze the similarities and differences. You might compare our Palestinian folktale "Ms. Cricket Gets Married" (p. 61) with *Perez and Martina* by Pura Belpré (Penguin 2004), a Puerto Rican story of a mouse who courts a cockroach. Each is a variant of the same folktale motif. One clear way to show these comparisons is by using hula hoops. Write down the elements of each story, label each hoop with a story title, then let the students place the elements in the spaces where they belong. Both tales are about courting. The suitor in each is a mouse. But one features a cockroach as the main female character, and the other is about a cricket. And there are many other differences.

Fluency and Expression

We want our students to be able to read books at their independent reading level with confidence, fluency, and expression. Students who have heard you giving voices to a variety of characters over the year will be better equipped to find a range of expression in their own voice as they read aloud to others. Children who have had experience telling their own stories will be better able to apply their understanding of speaking expressively in the context of reading a written text. Giving your students opportunities to record themselves while telling stories and then listening to their performance will help them set individual goals to become more expressive and fluent readers as the year progresses.

Speaking and Listening

Storytelling is a remarkable tool for helping students develop their speaking and listening skills. As we've already mentioned, the first time you share a tale with your class, we encourage you to tell it without interruption, with nothing to get in the way of the magic of the tale. When you share a story a second or third time, however, feel free to stop the story periodically and have your students "turn and talk" about pivotal moments. There are ample opportunities to have your students talk about stories and to listen to each other's opinions. Of course, when students learn to *tell* tales, they are able to take their speaking skills to a whole new level. Through sharing stories with others, they learn to speak clearly, with intention, and to care for their audience. In Chapter 7, we will focus in greater detail on the many benefits of turning your students into storytellers.

Effective communication requires listening as well as speaking. Storytelling is an important tool for developing your students' listening skills. A told story has no visual cues and the students must rely on their aural input to process the tale. And when they work in small groups to tell stories themselves, they learn to support each other with attentive listening.

Storytelling in a Digital Age

In our high-tech, modern world, oral storytelling is more relevant than ever before. Our students are growing up in a world that is increasingly defined by information and we need to give them the skills to manage and manipulate this information. We are now flooded with new and exciting digital tools to share our thinking in imaginative ways. We want our children to be able to use the latest technology to its best advantage, but what good is knowing *how* to make a fantastic digital presentation when you don't know *what* you want to say? The basis of every great digital game, movie or spectacle is a good story. A student who is confident in oral storytelling can develop a story worthy of any expressive format. Once they have the content, they can use technology to present it in exciting ways. Storytelling helps students develop and refine these crucial communication skills.

Let's Look at Grandfather Bear

Grandfather Bear is a perfect story to use to create a very simple type of pocket story.
1. Fold a piece of 8 ½ x 11 paper lengthwise. Now fold it up a third of the way from the bottom. Fold it down a third of the way from the top. Unfold.

2. Your paper now has six squares on it. Label them 1-6. Draw very simple icons in each square to help you remember the story sequence.

3. In square 1, draw a circle, two eyes, and two ears. This is Grandfather Bear.

4. In square 2, make five dots. These are the berries.

5. Square 3 gets 3 squiggles. This is the river.

6. In square 4, draw a rectangle on end. This is the stump.

7. For square 5, draw arrows up and down, up and down.

8. Finally, in square 6, draw 5 black lines to represent the chipmunk's stripes.

9. Fold the paper up and put it in your pocket. When you get home, you can take the pocket book out and use it to tell the story to someone!

For a text-to-text comparison see *How Chipmunk Got His Stripes* by Joseph Bruchac and James Bruchac, illustrated by Jose Aruego and Arianne Dewey (New York: Penguin, 2003.).

Try a Tale!

Of course *every* story is useful to connect with your Language Arts curriculum. We have selected two especially playful tales, with lots of language play. "Ms. Cricket Gets Married" is fun to act out and is an easy story to remember. "Teeny Weeny Bop" incorporates rhyming, which presents a perfect opportunity to let the children anticipate the rhyming word. This story also uses language play with invented words such as "jamster," showing that a teller is free to just make up words and PLAY with language!

Ms. Cricket Gets Married
A Palestinian-Arab Folktale.

Ms. Cricket wanted to get married.

"Momma, Momma! I want to get married!"

"Well then, go look for a husband," said her Momma.

Off went Ms. Cricket. Tzzz…tzzz…tzzz… *(she buzzes as she travels)*

There was Mr. Camel!

"Mr. Camel! Mr. Camel! Will you marry me?"

"Bah! Bah! You are nothing but a little CRICKET! A CRICKET!"

Ms. Cricket was incensed! "Cricket, Cricket yourself! Who do you think YOU are?"

Mr. Camel was impressed by her spunky attitude.

"Well, maybe I will marry you after all."

"Put your money in my sleeve," said Ms. Cricket. "And I'll go ask my Momma."

Tzzz…tzzz…tzzz…

"Momma! Momma! I have a suitor!"

"What is his name?"

"His name is Mr. CAMEL!"

"Mr. Camel? What does he look like?"

"Oh Momma I like the way he looks!

His head is very BIG

His nose is very BIG

His back is very BIG

He's BIG ALL OVER!"

"No! No! No! He would sit on you and squash you! Tell him NO!"

"Oooohhhh…" Ms. Cricket was disappointed. But back she went.

Tzzz…tzzz…tzzz…

"Mr. Camel, I can't marry you. You are TOO BIG!"

Tzzz…tzzz…tzzz…

There was Mr. Bull!

"Mr. BULL! Mr. BULL! Will you marry me?"

"BAH! BAH! You're nothing but a little CRICKET. A CRICKET!"

"Cricket, Cricket yourself! Who do you think YOU are?

Mr. Bull, too, was impressed by her spunky attitude.

"Well, maybe I'll marry you after all."

"Put your money in my sleeve, and I'll go ask my Momma."

Tzzz…tzzz…tzzz…

"Momma! Momma! I have a suitor!"

"What is his name?"

"His name is Mr. BULL!"

"Well, what does Mr. Bull look like?"

His head is very BIG

His nose is very BIG

His back is very BIG

He's BIG ALL OVER!"

"No! No! He would roll on you and squash you! Tell him NO!"

"Oooohhhh…"

Tzzz…tzzz…tzzz…

There was Mr. Mouse!

"Mr. MOUSE! Mr. MOUSE! Will you marry me?

"BAH! BAH! Why would I marry you?

You're nothing but a little CRICKET. A CRICKET!"

"Cricket, Cricket yourself! Who do you think YOU are?

Mr. Mouse was also impressed by her spunky attitude.

"Well, maybe I'll marry you after all."

"Put your money in my sleeve, and I'll go ask my Momma."

Tzzz…tzzz…tzzz…

Momma! Momma! I have a suitor!"

"What is his name?"

"His name is Mr. MOUSE!"

"Mr. Mouse? What does he look like?"

"I like the way he looks.

His head is very tiny.

His nose is very tiny.

His feet are very tiny.

He is TINY ALL OVER!"

"Oh, Ms. Cricket. That is the husband for you! He is just the right size. Marry him at once!"

So, Ms. Cricket and Mr. Mouse were married.

And lived happily ever after.

And all because she listened to her MOMMA!

Source: *Speak Bird, Speak Again: Palestinian Arab Folktales* by Ibrahim Muhawi and Sharif Kanaana. (Berkley: University of California Press, 1989). Retold in *Look Back and See: Twenty Lively Tales for Gentle Tellers* by Margaret Read MacDonald (New York: H.W. Wilson, 1991). See that source for other variants. This is *Motif Z37.3 Little Ant Finds a Penny, Buys New Clothes with It, and Sits in Her Doorway.* Compare our story with *Martina the Beautiful Cockroach: A Cuban Folktale* by Carmen Deedy, illus. by Michael Austin. (Atlanta: Peachtree, 2007).

Extending the Tale

- Learn about Palestine

- See "Ms. Cricket Does Her Laundry" in *Look Back and See: Twenty Lively Tales to Tell* by Margaret Read MacDonald (H.W. Wilson, 1991) to find out what happened *after* Ms. Cricket and Mr. Mouse were married!

- Discuss dowry traditions ("Put your money in my sleeve").

- Imagine what Ms. Cricket might have said to other suitors. Assign roles and act this story out. Create a song for Ms. Cricket to sing as she goes along. You could turn this little story into a mini-operetta.

- Share the story in Spanish. See www.margaretreadmacdonald.com for Spanish text.

The Teeny Weeny Bop
An Original Tale Expanded from British Folktale Motifs

One morning the Teeny Weeny Bop started sweeping her floor.
[You can have the children mime sweeping the floor as you do it.]
She was sweeping her floor and sweeping her floor and…
She found a gold coin stuck in a crack in her floor!
"My luck is MADE! I'll go to town and buy myself a little pet pig."

Off she went down the road…just a-singing!
[Have children pat their legs with you as you recite this chant. We usually make up a little tune to sing with it, too.]
   "To market! To market! To buy a fat pig!
   Home again! Home again! Jiggety-JIG!"

Got down to the market, went right up to the Pet Man.
"Mr. Pet Man, I want to trade my gold coin for a little pet pig."
"Gold coin for a pig? Good enough trade. Pick out any little pig you want."

She took the fattest little pig there. Started back up the road home just a-singing.
   "I went to market and I bought a fat pig!
   Now I'm coming home again, jiggety-JIG!"

When she got home, she wondered, "Where can I keep my pig?"
"I know. I'll lock him in the garden. He'll be safe in there."
She put him in the garden and closed the garden gate.
Then she went to bed…she went to sleep…she slept real sound.

Next morning Little Old Woman woke up.
"I wonder how my piggy got along last night?"
She hurried out to the garden and opened the garden gate.
"OH NO!" What do you think that pig had done during the night?

[Let the children tell you what happened. Any answer is correct. We finish with a rhyming refrain, but it is not necessary to use the rhyme. You can just take a variety of answers from the kids and say "Yes! That's just what he did!"]

He had rooted up her carrots.
He rooted up potatoes.
He rooted up her turnips.
Rooted all her rutabagas!

"PIG! PIG! What a MESS you've MADE!
I'm taking you to market and I'm going to TRADE!"

Said, "I'll take this pig back to market and trade for a better pet."
[Ask the children what pet you should get. Say you want a smaller pet.
They will call out lots of suggestions. Someone will say "cat."]

"That's a great idea! I'll get myself a CAT."

   "To market! To Market! To buy a fat CAT!
   Home again! Home again! Jiggety-JAT!"

"Mr. Pet Man, my pig made a mess of my garden! Can I trade my pig for a cat?"
"A pig for a cat? Good enough trade. Take any little cat you want."

"I'll take that little black and white one right there."

   "I went to market and I bought a fat CAT!
   Now I'm coming home again. Jiggety-JAT!"

"Where can I keep my little cat?
I'll just keep it right here in the living room. She'll be safe in here."
She went to bed…she went to sleep…and she slept real sound.

Next morning…
"Can't wait to see how my little cat did last night!"
Opened the living room door.
"OH NO!"
What do you think that cat had done during the night?
[Let them tell you what happened.]

Exactly!

She scratched the sofa.
She clawed the drapes.
She ripped the carpet.
She broke the vase!

"CAT! CAT! What a MESS you've MADE!
I'm taking you to market and I'm going to TRADE!"
[Tell your audience you want a smaller pet. Keep asking until someone suggests "hamster."]

Great idea!

"To Market! To Market! To buy a fat HAMSTER!
Home again! Home again! Jiggety-JAMSTER!"

"Mr. Pet Man! My cat tore up my living room. Can I trade my cat for a hamster?"

"Cat for a hamster? Good enough trade. Pick out any one you want."
"I'll take that fat little one right there!"

"I went to market and I bought a fat HAMSTER!
Now I'm coming home again. Jiggety-JAMSTER!"

"Now where will I keep my little pet hamster?
Can't let him run loose in the living room…
I KNOW! I'll keep him in the kitchen PANTRY! He'll be safe in there!"

She went to bed…she went to sleep…and she slept real sound.
Next morning…
"Wonder how my little hamster did during the night?"
Threw open that pantry door. "OH NO!"

What do you think that hamster had done?
[They will say "gnawed the cupboard," "ate the food," "broke the glasses," etc.]

Yes he HAD!

He ate up all the crackers.
He crunched the cornflakes.
He gnawed into the cookies.
He chomped into the cake.

"HAMSTER! HAMSTER! What a MESS you've MADE!
I'm taking you to market and I'm going to TRADE!"

"Let me see…I want something smaller.
I want a pet with no teeth, and no claws…

[Keep reiterating that you need a pet with no teeth, no claws, one that moves slowly. Someone will eventually suggest a snail.]

I know! A SLUG! A SLUG can't do any harm!"

   "To Market! To Market! To buy a fat SLUG!
   Home again! Home again! Gluggety-GLUG!"

"Mr. Pet Man, can I trade my hamster for a pet slug?"
"You want a SLUG?"
"Yes I want a pet that has no teeth and no claws and moves real slow. I saw you had some slugs on your plant over there."
"Hamster for a slug?" Good enough trade. Pick out any slug you want, ma'am."
"I want that really fat one right there!"
Slid that slug into her pocket and started along home.
   "I went to market and I bought a fat SLUG!
   Now I'm coming home again! Gluggety-GLUG!"

"Now where can I keep my little pet slug?
He likes it cool…and damp.
[Ask the kids where you should keep him. Keep saying cool, damp. Someone will finally say "refrigerator!"]

Perfect! I'll keep him in the refrigerator! He'll be safe in there!"
She put that slug in her refrigerator. Shut the door.
She went to bed…she went to sleep…she slept real sound.

Next morning she ran out there to see how her slug had done.

Yanked open that refrigerator door.

"OH NO!"

What do you think that slug had done during the night?

[Some will say he ate the food, but some will know that he slimed things.]

He slimed the butter.

He slimed the cheese.

He slimed the Jell-O.

He slimed the peas.

"SLUG! SLUG! What a MESS you've MADE!

I'm taking you to market and I'm going to TRADE!"

Said, "These pets are just NOT working out. I'm going to trade for my gold coin back.

"To market! To market! To get my gold coin!

To market! To market! To get my gold coin!"

"Mr. Pet Man, I want to trade my slug back for my gold coin."

"Say what, Ma'am? I can't give you a gold coin for a slug."

"Oh. Well, then I'll trade my slug for my PIG back."

"No way, Ma'am. I can't give you a pig for a slug."

"Well then give me my CAT back."

"Sorry, Ma'am. Can't trade a cat for a slug either.

"Could I have my HAMSTER back then?"

"Ma'am your slug is not worth anything. I can't give you a hamster for a slug."

"Well this doesn't seem right. I had a gold coin a while ago.

Then I had a PIG...then I had a CAT...then I had a HAMSTER...

And now all I've got left is a SLUG. And I don't even want it. You can have it back."

"I went to market and I couldn't even trade.

I went to market and I couldn't even trade."

She went home so sad.

After a while she decided she'd better do her housework.

Got up and started sweeping her floor. Sweeping her floor and sweeping her floor and…

[Children sweep with you.]

"AHA!" She found a SILVER coin stuck in a crack in the floor!

"MY LUCK IS MADE! I'll go back to town and buy myself another pet!

Think I'll buy myself a BIG FAT HOG!"

> "To Market! To Market! To buy a fat HOG!
> Home Again! Home Again! Jiggety-JOG!"

No more! No more! Teeny Weeny Bop!

Your silly story has got to…STOP!

[If you pause, the audience will supply the word STOP for you.]

Source: For a picture book version of this story with illustrations by Dianne Greenseid, see *Teeny Weeny Bop*, Margaret Read MacDonald (Morton Grove, IL: Albert Whitman Company, 2006). There is an earlier version in *Look Back and See: Twenty Lively Tales for Gentle Tellers* (New York: H.W. Wilson, 1991). This is an original tale created from British folktale motifs and inspired by a story by Australian teller Jean Chapman. The folktale motifs included are *Motif J2081.1 Foolish bargain: horse for cow, cow for hog, etc. Finally nothing left.* And *Motif Z41.5 Lending and repaying: progressively worse (or better) bargain.*

About Telling the Story

We often tell the story without using the rhyming couplets. Those were created for the picture book version of the story, and we think they sound fun, so we have put them in here. If you don't want to worry about memorizing those, leave them out. It is fun to just let the audience give you possibilities for what the animal might have done and then say, "That's exactly what he did! Cat! What a mess you've made! I'm taking you to market and I'm going to TRADE!"

Extending the Tale

This is a fun story to act out. Try it several times and give students a chance to play with the story.

- What other animals might she have traded for and what sort of trouble would they have caused?

- Think about the value of items. What causes some to be worth more than others?

- Set up a pet store to sell animal cut-outs. Establish fixed prices for each animal and create paper money in a variety of denominations, including gold coins. Be sure the purchaser gets proper change for their gold coin when they buy something.

Ready…Set…Tell!

Think about your school's language expectations. How could you use storytelling to support language instruction in your context? Choose one reading strategy that you are focusing on with your class. Find a story that will help you develop that skill orally and try it out this week! Choose a story to tell and then have your students make a pocket story to carry the tale home.

Chapter 4: CURRICULUM— Enlivening and Expanding Curriculum with Story

"If history were taught in the form of stories, it would never be forgotten."

— Rudyard Kipling

A well-placed story can energize any area of your curriculum. Because ideas and facts are best remembered when ingrained with emotion, storytelling is an effective device for connecting the student to your curriculum. Storytelling has many clear links to literacy, language, and the creative arts and we have devoted entire chapters to those areas in this book. We want to emphasize, though, that story can be linked to ANY area of instruction and is equally useful when connected with math and science, or health and physical education. As educators, we often look for ways to integrate subjects and help students make connections across disciplines. Storytelling offers a perfect avenue for integration. In this chapter, we will offer suggestions for ways to use story in a variety of subject areas across your school curriculum.

> *The teaching tales I've used so far get much more response from the students than if I had taught the concept directly. They act as if they've personally learned the point by participating in the story.*
>
> — Kathy McConnell, Grade 1, Dorothy Fox Elementary, Camas, WA.

History

Storyteller Gerry Fierst once told us the gripping tale of an evil-hearted King who lived in a castle along the Rhine River in Germany. In the story, the king flees from a horde of rats by locking himself up in a small tower on an island in the middle of the river. He winds up being devoured by the rats—a fitting end for the greedy king. When Gerry told this story, the details were vivid in our minds. We could see the castle on the hill and the tower in the river clearly. Years later, we were traveling down the Rhine River and saw a tower in the middle of the river. The story of the king came instantly to mind and when we started talking about it, we were amazed that we could recall the entire story in sharp detail. As we strolled along the riverside park, we found a sign that said we were looking at the

"Mouse Tower" and there was a brief summary of the same story. If we had read that story years earlier in a book or magazine, we're sure we would not have remembered it in the same way. It was the emotion linked with Gerry's riveting telling of the story that lodged the information in our minds.

Storytelling can offer this same "staying power" for any bits of historical information you would like to share with your students. Many teachers find ways to tell the stories of the historical characters that are important to their field. Think back on your own education. You can probably think of certain teachers who were skilled at bringing historical characters and events to life through narrative. Telling the tales of Archimedes or Genghis Khan or Galileo or Harriet Tubman, rather than simply reading about them, will stir excitement in your students and draw them into a personal relationship with history. Once students have grasped a sense of storytelling, they can use this technique to present their understanding of history. Giving students the freedom to present their history reports as stories can help them connect with their subject on a deeper level. Rather than writing a paper full of facts about a key historical figure, why not enable your students to gather facts and then tell the story of that important character? History can come alive for the entire class through the stories of its actors. Many teachers have had luck with demonstrating the telling of a biographical story from history and then assisting their students in researching their own stories to perform in character as the historical figure they have chosen. Kevin Cordi and Sherry and Bobby Norfolk, share their experiences with these kinds of learning engagements in *The Storytelling Classroom: Applications Across the Curriculum* by Sherry Norfolk, Jane Stenson, and Diane Williams (Westport, CT: Libraries Unlimited, 2006), p. 171-179.

Geography

Look for stories to connect to your studies of world places. Tales often contain information about climate, environment, landscape. "The Elephants and the Bees" takes place during a forest fire in Thailand's northern, mountainous region. "Little Basket Weaver" is set in the Northwestern U.S. rain forest. "Grandfather Bear" leads the listener on a wander through a Siberian spring mountainside. Sharing a story from the landscape you are studying can create intimacy and connection to the place.

Social Issues

Story can be a great discussion starter when examining social issues. Share the story of "Two Goats on a Bridge" (p. 162) to open a discussion of pathways to peace. Share "Not Our Problem" (p. 29) when you talk about responsibility for ecological disasters. Use "Old

Man Wombat" (p. 106) to consider treatment of the elderly and infirm. Tell "Frog and Locust Call for Rain" (p. 172) when you talk about cooperation to forward a cause. And "Monkeys in the Rain" (p. 170) can remind everyone to start working on these important issues today!

To lead discussions of pathways to war and pathways to peace, we suggest *Peace Tales: World Folktales to Talk About* (Margaret Read MacDonald, Atlanta: August House, 2006). Margaret found it difficult to find folktales on pathways to peace. Our cultures have fostered tales of competition, tricksters, and quests for gold, power, or princesses. But not so many tales have been told of kindness, sharing, and peacemaking. Perhaps it is time to begin telling those stories. Watch for good tales that promote peace and goodwill and share them.

The told story is also a fine way to get children thinking about our earth and its needs. *Earth Care: World Folktales to Talk About* (Margaret Read MacDonald, Atlanta: August House, 2005) offers 35 stories about man's relationship to the land. It was easy for Margaret to find these stories because almost every people who lived close to the earth developed cautionary tales to warn their children of the dangers of taking too many animals, too many fish, of cutting too many trees. We need their folk wisdom to guide us today and remind us of the necessity of conservation. These peoples knew that their lives depended on treating the earth well. You can use these stories to help your students ponder the ways we can help heal our planet.

Story is also useful in thinking about justice. Share stories of wise judges such as King Solomon and the Japanese Ooka the Wise. Watch for stories that show conflicts being resolved wisely. Find stories about heroes aiding the downtrodden. One useful book is *The Cow of No Color: Riddle Stories and Justice Tales from Around the World* by Nina Jaffe and Steve Zeitlin (New York: Henry Holt, 1998).

Math

Math and storytelling? Of course! Wrapping a math problem in an engaging story involves the child's brain on multiple levels. It's also a great way to engage those students who gravitate toward verbal activities. Using story to explore math problems gives you other tools to connect with math: dramatization, puppetry, artwork, musical motifs.

There are many math-related folktales told by cultures around the world. We start with one of our favorites, and then suggest more tales for math-connection possibilities. There are so many ways to utilize a good story in math instruction—you just need to open yourself to the possibilities!

Counting to Ten
A Math Riddle

King Leopard needed to choose an heir to take over the throne.

He decided to have a contest.

"Whoever can throw this spear into the air while dancing and count to ten before it falls back into his hand…*he* shall be the new prince of the kingdom."

All of the animals came to compete.

Elephant tried. He threw the spear as hard as he could and began to count.

"One…Two…Three…" The spear fell back to earth.

Ox tried.

"One…Two…Three…Four…" The spear hit the ground.

Many animals tried. All animals failed. No one could throw the spear high enough so that he could count to ten before the spear fell back to earth.

Then Little Deer came forward.

"I would like to try, Your Honor."

Everyone laughed. How could such a tiny creature accomplish the task?

But Little Deer picked up the spear and THREW it into the air—and won the contest.

How is this possible?

Answer: She counted by 5's. "Five, Ten!"

This is a simple retelling of the well-known tale. You can expand it, act it out, play with it, and extend it in multiple ways. Are there other ways that Deer could have counted to 10? What if the animals had to count to 20? 50? What are some of the other ways they could have counted? This is a story that lends itself well to acting out quickly and retelling in small groups.

Our story is elaborated from "The New Prince" in George Shannon's *More Stories to Solve* (Greenwillow, 2001). For a picture-book version of this story see *Two Ways to Count to Ten: A Liberian Folktale*. Retold by Ruby Dee. Illus. by Susan Meddaugh (New York: Henry Holt, 1988).

There are many ways to integrate story into mathematics instruction. What follows is a list of ideas and suggested tales organized by mathematical strand.

Numbers and Operations

It is easy to take a story like "The Squeaky Door" (p. 158) and use it in the primary class-rooms to explore number concepts. What if there were two pigs, three cats, and four dogs tucked in with the little boy? How many animals would there be altogether? You can act out the story, use counters to tell the story, and write number sentences to represent the mathematical thinking in the story. Tell and retell the story in small groups with different numbers of animals each time to create new number sentences. It is possible to deepen understanding of a mathematical concept through a story that is already well-loved by the class.

Jen uses the story "Too Much Noise" to think about numbers with her kindergarteners. In this story a man complains that his home is too noisy. A wise man tells him to bring a cat into the house, then a dog, etc. At last, the house is *really* noisy and he is told to take them away. On the first day of teaching the unit, Jen told the story. The next day she let them act the story out, while introducing mathematical language: "How many _____? "How many altogether?" "How many are left?" The following day the students retold the story placing paper animal cutouts in a circle on the floor. She asked, "Now how many does the man have?" Students shared their strategies for discovering the correct answer.

After reviewing the story on the fourth day, each child was given a set of animals to color and cut out. They then paired with a classmate to retell the story. They could put as many animals as they liked in the house. They were encouraged to write their number sentences down as they told their stories: 2 dogs + 3 cats = 5 animals in the house. Students then took their animals home to share the story with their families.

Many versions of this story are available, for example:

Too Much Noise by Ann McGovern, Illustrated by Simms Taback. Sandpiper, 1992; "What a Wonderful Life!" in *Shake-it-up Tales* by Margaret Read MacDonald, August House, 2000; *A Big Quiet House* by Heather Forest, Illustrated by Susan Greenstein, August House, 2005.

Ways of Counting

The following tales deal with different methods of counting:

"Punia and the King of the Sharks" in *Twenty Tellable Tales: Audience Participation Folktales for the Beginning Storyteller*. By Margaret Read MacDonald (New York: H.W. Wilson, 1986). In this Hawaiian tale, Punia tells the King of the Sharks that it was the first...then the second...then the third shark that told Punia how to fool the King of the Sharks. Punia counts to the tenth shark.

How Many Spots Does a Leopard Have? And Other Tales. By Julius Lester. Illus. by David Shannon (New York: Scholastic, 1989), p. 53-57. Leopard has just two spots, white and black. But the tale employs lots of counting attempts and even multiplication on the way to figuring that out.

How Many Donkeys? An Arabic Counting Tale. Retold by Margaret Read MacDonald and Nadia Jameel Taiba. Illus. by Carol Liddiment (Chicago: Albert Whitman, 2009). A man fails to count the donkey he is riding on. He counts to ten in Arabic repeatedly.

Addition

Some tales that allow students to practice adding include:

"Frog and Locust" (p. 172). Keep adding frogs and locusts and asking "How many now?"

"The Squeaky Door" (p. 158). Have the children act the roles of animals being tucked into bed. Add in two dogs, three cats, etc.

Farmyard Jamboree by Margaret Read MacDonald. Illus. by Sophie Fatus (New York: Barefoot Books, 2011). In this Chilean folktale, two animals (a mother and a baby) are added with each verse. Add them up and find the total number of animals at the end of the story. Also available in Spanish: *Algarabía en la Granja* (New York Barefoot Books, 2009).

Multiplication

The King's Chessboard by David Birch, illus. Devis Grebu, (Puffin Books, 1993) tells the story of a clever man who requests as reward from the king that a grain of rice be placed in one square of a chessboard, and that the amount in each square be doubled in the next square. The story is often told of the inventor of the chessboard. For discussion of many variants of this tale, along with mathematical formula see: en.wikipedia.org/wiki/Wheat_and_chessboard_problem.

One Grain of Rice: A Mathematical Folktale by Aliki (Scholastic, 1997) retells this tale about a girl in India who asks for double the amount of rice each day for a month. You can stop the tale and have students work out how many grains of rice will be presented to the girl on the last day of the month.

"Nine Bamboo Clumps" in *Lao Folktales* by Wajuppa Tossa and Kongdeuane Nettavong (Libraries Unlimited, 2008), p. 63-64. Nine bamboo clumps, nine bamboo stems each, nine sections to each stem, nine bees in each section. How many bees?

"The Magic Doubling Pot" is a favorite tale of a pot that instantly doubles anything that is put inside. You can find a tellable version in Pleasant DeSpain's *Thirty-Three Multicultural Tales to Tell* (Atlanta, August House, 1993), p. 71-73. Lily Toy Hong also has a lovely picture book version called *Two of Everything* (Albert Whitman, 1993). Students can retell this story and include different numbers of items that are put into the pot. Children can also make a magic pot book, drawing in objects and then doubling and re-doubling them. Older children could make it a magic tripling pot or a magic squaring pot.

The Magic Pot is an easy-to-read Story Cove picture book adaptation of this story, by Pleasant DeSpain, Illustrated by Tom Wrenn (Atlanta: August House, 2007).

Division

"Fighting Leads to Losses" in *Peace Tales: World Folktales to Talk About* by Margaret Read MacDonald (Atlanta: August House, 2005), p. 34. In this tale from India, two otters fight over one fish. Jackal divides it for them, giving the top to one, and the bottom to other. The choicest middle part is for the judge.

"A Question of Arithmagic" in the *Crystal Pool: Myths and Legends of the World*. Retold by Geraldine McCaughrean. Illus. by Bea Willey (Margaret K. McElderry Books, 1999), p. 14-17. In this Icelandic tale King Olaf is accosted by an old man (a troll in disguise) who will not let the king's ship pass the cliffs. The troll poses a riddle: "If there are twelve ships, each with twelve crew members, and each kills a dozen seals, and each skin is cut into twelve pieces, and then cut again, and each piece will serve ten men, how many men are there? While Olaf tries to figure out the riddle, the ship is almost wrecked.

Fractions

In "Ooka and the Two First Sons" each of two men claims half of a group of thirteen horses. A judge bets two other judges that he can solve the dispute. To do so, he adds the other judges' horses to the original thirteen horses and divides the total in two, giving seven horses to each man. Then he takes the remaining horse as his payment. This tale is found in *Ooka the Wise: Tales of Old Japan* by I.G. Edmonds (Bobbs-Merrill, 1961), p. 81-86.

"Molla Nasreddin and His Donkey" tells of three men who buy 17 donkeys. One man pays half the price, one pays one-third, and one pays one-ninth. Mullah adds his donkey, making 18 donkeys in all, then he divides them: The first man gets nine donkeys, the second man gets six, and the last one gets two. Mullah takes back his own donkey. This Iranian folktale can be found in *Eurasian Folk and Fairy Tales* by I. F. Bulatkin (Criterion, 1965), p. 64-68.

In the Jamaican tale "Anansi and the Plantains" Anansi gives one of four plantains to each member of his family, keeping none for himself. They each give him back half of their plantains, as he has none, so Anansi ends up with two plantains and his family members each have only a half. Find this tale in Philip M. Sherlock's *Anansi the Spiderman* (Crowell, 1954) p. 64-69.

"Half gone" tells how Cat and Mouse store a jar of butter together. Cat goes to a christening and when he comes back, he says that the child was named "Just begun." The next day, he reports that another child was named "Half Gone." Finally, Cat tells Mouse about the child named "All Gone." This tale can be found in most editions of *Grimm's Fairy Tales*. There is an African American version in *The People Could Fly* by Virginia Hamilton (Knopf, 2009), p. 13-19.

Estimation

"Just a Little More" in *Earth Care: World Folktales to Talk About* by Margaret Read Mac-Donald (August House, 2005) is a Portuguese folktale retold by Greg Goggins about a man who is given all the land he can walk around before sunset. He fails to estimate correctly, and so he loses all. You could set up your own math problem: If the man is given a field 100 x 100 feet and he can walk 10 feet per minute, can he cover all of the land if he walks for 60 minutes?

"The Red Brick Temple" in *Three Minute Tales* by Margaret Read MacDonald (August House, 2004), p. 143, is a Thai tale. A man asks an old woman, "How long will it take to reach the temple?" He is answered, "I do not know." As the man starts walking toward the temple the woman calls out the answer, "Two hours." She had to see how fast he was walking before she could estimate how long it would take him to reach the temple. You can create a math problem from this. For example, if he is walking one mile per hour, how far away is the temple?

Data and Probability

Nancy Ishigaki, of Kent, Washington, used the familiar folktale "Stone Soup" to help her students explore data collection. After telling the story, Nancy had her students ask at home about favorite soup ingredients. The students came back with a list of things to put in soup and Nancy then guided her students in graphing these ingredients. From these graphs came the familiar data questions. Which ingredients were used most? Which least? She did this graphically, but suggests that using colored blocks to represent the various ingredients would be another way to help them understand comparisons. There are many variants of this story, *Motif K112.2 "Soup Stone" wins hospitality.* See: *Stone Soup* by Heather Forest. Illus. by Susan Gaber (Atlanta: August House, 2005); *Stone Soup* by Ann McGovern. Illus. Winslow Pinney Pel (New York: *Scholastic*, 1986); *Stone Soup* by Marcia Brown (New York: Aladdin, 1997); "Nail Soup" in *Celebrate the World: Twenty Tellable Folktales for Multicultural Festivals* by Margaret Read MacDonald (New York: H.W. Wilson, 1994).

Measurement

Tamra Bruner, a teacher in Chattaroy, Washington, used the folktale "The Line" from George Shannon's *Still More Stories to Solve* (Greenwillow, 1996), p. 10-12, in her sixth-grade math class. The story tells how Birbal solves a riddle posed by the Moghul Emperor Akbar. "Make this line shorter." Birbal accomplishes this by simply drawing a longer line beside the first. After trying this out, Tammy wrote, "I can't believe some of the answers I was getting from my students with this riddle. They really pulled from our Math instruction on "lines" to come up with answers on how Birbal had accomplished the impossible task of making the line drawn by the Emperor Akbar shorter. What a great activity to do with our Math unit on lines and line segments. I will definitely use this in the years to come."

Two Foolish Cats by Yoshiko Uchida. Illus. by Margot Zemach (Margaret K. McElderry, 1987) is a Japanese tale of two cats quarreling over rice cakes. One rice cake is bigger than the other, so Monkey weighs them in his scale, then nibbles the cakes till they are the same weight.

In "The Cat and the Rat" in *A Ring of Tricksters* by Virginia Hamilton (Blue Sky Press, 1997), p. 33-37, a Gullah tale from Georgia, Cat and Rat argue over which half of a piece of cheese is bigger. Fox weighs the cheese and cuts off pieces—for the judge—to make the portions even.

"The Peasant and His Plot" in *The Family Storytelling Handbook* by Anne Pellowski, (MacMillan, 1987), p. 64-66. Farmer's square plot of land with one tree at each corner. Farmers can have more land *if* they keep their land in a square and keep their trees where they are, but trees still must be on the edge of the plot. Daughter solves the problem.

Money

"Pig and Bear in Business" is included at the end of this chapter. In this story, Pig and Bear go into business together, but they eat up each other's stock.

"The Teeny Weeny Bop" (p. 64) shows how Teeny Weeny Bop learns the relative value of items by finding out what makes a good trade.

Complicated Math Tale

"How Many Geese? A Latvian Riddle Tale" in *Five Minute Tales* by Margaret Read Mac-Donald (August House, 2007), p. 83, presents a math problem that requires several calculations. A man says that he has a flock of one hundred geese. The lead goose in the flock says that number isn't correct, but that, if you double the number of geese in the flock, add half of that number to the total, and then add one-fourth of the number of geese in the flock to that, and add one, then that number would be one hundred. How many geese were in the original flock?

Share the Stories of Famous Mathematicians

Tell the stories of famous mathematicians and their discoveries. Kendall Haven provides samples of this sort of story in his *Marvels of Math: Fascinating Reads and Awesome Activities* (Teacher Ideas Press, 1998).

Sources for Using Storytelling in the Math Curriculum:

Dacy, Linda and Rebeka Eston. *Show and Tell: Representing and Communicating Mathematical Ideas in K-1 Classrooms* (Sausalito, CA: Math Solutions Publications, 2002), p. 39-49. This book provides a detailed account of how her kindergarteners discovered how many hands were needed to pull out a giant watermelon by making drawings to record their counting efforts. It could be used when telling the Russian tale of "The Enormous Turnip."

Norfolk, Sherry with Jane Stenson and Diane Williams. *The Storytelling Classroom: Applications Across the Curriculum* (Westport, CT: Libraries Unlimited, 2006). Included are a few suggestions for math-story connections.

Whittin, Phyllis and David. *Math is Language Too: Talking and Writing in the Mathematics Classroom* (Urbana, Ill: National Council of Teachers of English, 2000), p. 18-25. They suggest many ways to explore the riddle tale "Counting to Ten" (p. 74).

Zakis, Rina and Peter Lijedahl. *Teaching Mathematics as Storytelling* (Rotterdam: Sense Publishers, 2009). These Canadian authors from Simon Fraser University suggest many story problems to use with grades one through nine. Some are quite complicated and probably most useful for upper elementary through high school students.

Science

A story can make a great introduction to a science unit. It stimulates thought about the topic and gives you a hook for discussion. You can discover stories on a variety of science topics by checking the subject index in *The Storyteller's Sourcebook* by Margaret Read MacDonald (Gale Research, 1982; supplement by Margaret Read MacDonald and Brian Sturm, 2001) or see the resources listed below, which include many good story connections. Again, there are multiple ways to link stories with science instruction. Here are a few ideas to get you started.

Motion

The Panamanian story *Conejito*, in a picture book by Margaret Read MacDonald (August House, 2006), tells the story of a little rabbit who escapes Tiger, Lion, and Fox by rolling down a hill in a barrel. Ines Zerbato of Talbot Hill Elementary in Kent, Washington, used this story to help her students think about motion. Their science project included rolling marbles from different heights and angles using a tube. After telling the story, she demonstrated the motion described in the story by putting a toy bunny in a can and rolling him down a ramp. The story connection helped her students imprint the concept.

Pulleys

A discussion of pulleys could be enhanced by sharing the Brer Rabbit story, "That's the Way the World Goes." When Brer Fox jumps into one bucket hanging from the well's pulley, the lighter Brer Rabbit, who was stuck down in the well, rises in the second bucket and is rescued, while the fox is left in the well. "That's the Way the World Goes" is found in *Five Minute Tales* by Margaret Read MacDonald (August House, 2007).

Plants

To introduce the discussion of the properties of different types of plants, try one of the many variants on the story of the trickster who takes the tops of the corn, and bottoms of the carrots. See *Tops and Bottoms* by Janet Stevens (Harcourt, 1995) in which Hare tricks Bear. Peter Asbjørnsen and Jørgen Moe's *East of the Sun and West of the Moon* (any edition) has a Norwegian variant. For a Native American version, see p. 25-31 in Diane Goode's *The Diane Goode Book of American Folk Tales and Songs* (Puffin, 1996). An African American version, "Bruh Wolf and Bruh Rabbit Join Together" appears on p. 39-43 in Virginia Hamilton's *A Ring of Tricksters* (Blue Sky Press, 1997).

Tree Species

The Estonian tale of "Mikku and the Trees" in *Earth Care: World Folktales to Talk About* by Margaret Read MacDonald (August House, 2005, p. 22-27) tells of a woodcutter who is told by each tree, "I am useful because…" The woodcutter spares each tree and is rewarded with a magic wand, which he later misuses by asking for something that goes against the ways of nature. Teachers have found this story useful for talking about our relationship to the forest. Several have let their students dramatize the tale. Students need not memorize lines; just let them improvise the action once they know the story. Fourth graders at Tianjin International School gave Margaret a delightful performance of this tale, adding trees native to China to make the story even more meaningful.

Recycling

There is a well-known Jewish tale of a tailor who keeps reusing his coat, vest and cap, to make ever smaller useful clothing items. He ends up with a button—which still has just enough material to "make this story." An easy-to-tell version is "The Tailor's Jacket" in *Earth Care: World Folktales to Talk About* by Margaret Read MacDonald (Atlanta: August House, 1999).

Sun

In the Chinese tale "The Sun Sisters" in *Three Minute Tales* by Margaret Read MacDonald (August House, 2004), p. 14, sisters who live on the sun embroider. They will poke their needles in your eyes if you look at them. This story can be used as a warning not to look directly at the sun. Another timeless story that incorporates the sun is *Contest Between Sun and the Wind* by Heather Forest and Illustrated by Susan Gaber (August House, 2008). An Aesop Fable that demonstrates elements of weather, especially the interplay between the sun and the wind.

Changes in Matter

To introduce a discussion of how atmospheric moisture condenses as dew on cool nights, try the riddle, "Three Rosebushes" in which a spell allows a wife to spend nights with her husband, but she turns into a rosebush by day. If the husband can tell which of three identical bushes is his wife, she will be free of the spell. He goes out first thing in the morning, just after she leaves, and identifies her as the rosebush with no dew on it. In George Shannon's *Stories to Solve* (Greenwillow, 2000) p. 30.

Senses

There are several versions of a tale about a man who requires payment from a person who merely *smelled* his food. The judge rules that he be paid with only the *sound* (clink) of money. Find an Iranian version in Alice Kelsey's *Once the Mullah* (McKay, 1954), p. 122-127; a Peruvian rendition can be found in Jeanne Hardendorff's *Frog's Saddle Horse* (Lippincott, 1968),

p. 29-39; and an Italian variant is in Domenico Vittorini's *The Thread of Life: Twelve Old Italian Tales* (Crown, 1995), p. 15-18.

Body

There are several tales that deal with body parts. In "Who Obeys Stomach?" the body parts argue over which is most important—and the stomach wins. It can be found in Tom Paxton's *Belling the Cat and Other Aesop Fables* (Morrow, 1988), as well as in several other collections of Aesop's fables.

In "What is the Most Important Part of the Body?" in Julius Lester's, *How Many Spots Does a Leopard Have?* (Scholastic, 1989), p. 45-51, stomach is, at first, named the most important part, but tongue saves the whole body by speaking cleverly to the king. So, tongue is determined to be the most important part of the body.

In the picture book *Head, Body, Legs* by Margaret H. Lippert and Won-Ldy Paye, illustrated by Julie Paschkis (Holt, 2005), Head can't reach the cherries high up on the cherry tree until it teams up with the arms. The body tries to help, but it takes the legs to get them all to reach the mangoes.

Tell the Stories of Famous Scientists

Read about the lives of famous scientists and prepare short biographic tales to share with your students. Look for interesting details that will help your students connect with these important figures from the past. For example, did you know that Galileo's early study of pendulums was inspired by observing the motion of a chandelier swinging in a cathedral as a teenager? Small moments like these humanize our great thinkers from the past and show students that their personal observations today can spark important discoveries tomorrow. Kendall Haven demonstrates this sort of short story in his *Marvels of Science: 50 Fascinating Reads* (Libraries Unlimited, 1994).

Resources Connecting Story and Science

Bruchac, Joseph and Michael Caduto. *Keepers of the Earth: Native American Stories and Environmental Activities for Children.* (Golden, CO: Fulcrum, 1997). This collection of retellings of Native American tales, each with extensive environmental activities to accompany the story is part of a series by these co-authors.

Lipke, Barbara. *Figures, Facts and Fables: Telling Tales in Science and Math* (Portsmouth, NH: Heinemann, 1996)

MacDonald, Margaret Read. *Earth Care: World Folktales to Talk About* (Atlanta, GA: August House, 2005). Folktales are on themes of caretaking our earth.

Moroney, Lynn. *Moon Tellers: Myths of the Moon from Around the World* (Lanham, MD: Cooper Square Publishing, 1995). Twelve tales from twelve cultures show what people see when they look at the moon.

Strauss, Kevin. *Tales with Tails: Storytelling the Wonders of the Natural World* (Westport, CT: Libraries Unlimited, 2006). This book includes ideas for using stories in environmental education and a list of stories to use, along with their sources. Strauss's versions of many tales are included, with suggestions for their use in science activities.

Emotional Health

Researchers in bibliotherapy find that story can work to soothe and help the individual make sense of traumatic events. It doesn't matter if the story is heard before, during, or after the event, a benefit still can be felt. Story can also be a way to open avenues for discussion of difficult issues. Storyteller Myrna Ann Hecht from Vashon Island, Washington, shares the story of "Orpheus and Eurydice" to help students begin to write and talk about loss. See her article, "Myth and Poetry in the Middle School Classroom: Springboards for Telling and Writing about Loss" in *The Storytelling Classroom: Applications Across the Curriculum* by Sherry Norfolk, Jane Stenson, and Diane Williams (Westport, CT: Libraries Unlimited, 2006), p. 159-162. Erica Helm Meade, a psychologist and storyteller, also from Vashon Island, Washington, uses story to help troubled girls and women. She tells of her work in *Tell it by Heart: Women and the Healing Power of Story* (Chicago: Open Court, 1995).

Allison Cox and David H. Alpert provide stories and discussion of the uses of story in the maintenance and building of community in *The Healing Heart for Communities: Storytelling for Strong and Healthy Communities* (Gabriola Island, B.C.: New Society, 2003). They provide stories and discussion of the use of story to support healthy family life in *The Healing Heart for Families: Storytelling to Encourage Caring and Healthy Families* (Gabriola Island, B.C.: New Society, 2003).

You may also find it useful to explore *The Uses of Enchantment* by psychologist Bruno Bettelheim (Vintage, 2010). He speaks strongly about the importance of frightening tales in the emotional life of the child. It is through hearing such tales and working through the fears they bring up that the child learns that he also can encounter real-life monsters and survive.

Physical Education

Many stories can provide opportunities to introduce the day's activities in Physical Education classes. A short tale piques the students' imaginations and prepares them for the work ahead.

Before introducing forward rolls and log rolls to her young students, physical therapist Tamara Osborn shared the story of *Head, Body, Legs* by Margaret Lippert and Won-Ldy Paye (Holt, 2005). In the tale, a rolling head acquires its body parts while rolling all over the place.

To work on stretching and strengthening abdominal muscles, Tamara used "Lifting the Sky" (p. 187). In this Native American tale, all work together to push up the sky with poles. The audience participates in pushing toward the sky. Tamara was also interested in teaching her students the concept of working together, which is demonstrated in the story.

The Balinese teller Made Taro invited Margaret to the garden where he teaches children each Saturday. That day he told them the Aesop Fable of stork and fox. Stork invites fox to dinner and feeds him food in a tall vase. Fox cannot reach the food. Fox then invites stork for dinner and feeds him soup on a flat plate. Stork cannot pick up the food. Made Taro then set a tall vase at one end of the garden and gave the students tongs. Working in relay teams, they had to lift a bean from the vase, run the length of the garden, deposit the bean on a plate, and hand off the tongs to the next runner. This story is found in most collections of Aesop's Fables.

Many PE teachers have used "Two Goats on a Bridge" (p. 162) to help their students think about cooperation. And it also makes a nice lead-in to balance beam activities.

These are just a few examples of ways that story can excite children about physical activity. We've worked in schools in which the Art, PE, and Music teachers teamed up to bring stories alive through visual art, movement, and music. Find a story you love then let your imagination go wild in planning how to connect it to physical activity.

Folktales that Feature Athletic Activities

Another way to connect with story is to tell a tale featuring the activity you plan for the day. For example:

Soccer:

Bat's Big Game by Margaret Read MacDonald, illus. by Eugenia Nobati (Chicago: Albert Whitman, 2008). In a game between the animals and birds, Bat wants to win above all else. First, he joins the animal team, then switches to the bird team. The tale ends with Bat receiving a lesson on sportsmanship. *Motif B261.1 Bat in war between birds and quadrupeds.*

Tug of War:

"Tug-of-War" in *How Many Spots Does a Leopard Have? And Other Tales* by Julius Lester (Scholastic, 1989), p. 17-20. A tiny trickster arranges a tug-of-war between two large animals, in this case a turtle pits an elephant and a hippo against each other. This story is also in *Thirty-Three Multicultural Tales to Tell* by Pleasant DeSpain (August House, 1993) and it can be found in many collections with varying characters. *Motif K22 Deceptive Tug of War.*

Anansi and the Tug O' War by Bobby and Sherry Norfolk, illustrated by Baird Hoffmire (Atlanta: August House, 2007). This Story Cove picture book adaptation of an Anansi story from Africa, shows how strength is not as important as resourcefulness and respect in resolving differences.

Foot Race:

The Tortoise and the Hare: An Aesop Fable by Janet Stevens (Holiday House, 1985). This Aesop fable is retold in many picture books and collections. *Motif K11.3 Hare and Tortoise Race.*

Atalanta's Race: A Greek Myth by Shirley Climo, illustrated by Alexander Koshkin (Sandpiper, 2000). A girl wins a race by tossing a golden apple behind her. *H331.5.1.1 Apple thrown in race with bride.*

"Horse and Toad" in *The Magic Orange Tree and Other Haitian Folktales* by Diane Wolkstein (Schocken, 1997), p. 143-150. Toad places a relative at each milepost to make it seem that he has run the entire race, and then he waits at the finish line. There are many versions of this motif, from all over the world. *Motif K11.1 Race won by deception: Relative helpers.*

When Turtle Grew Feathers, A Folktale from the Choctaw Nation by Tim Tingle and illustrated by Stacey Schuett (Atlanta: August House, 2007). In this native tale from the Choctaw Nation, we learn that it was not slow and steady that helped Turtle win the big race with the Hare but resourcefulness.

Testing and Assessments

Telling a short story during your school's testing cycle is a great way to relax your students and take their minds to a more pleasant place for a few moments. Here is how one teacher used storytelling on testing day.

Today, my students are taking the writing MSP (our state standardized test). After lunch I decide to tell a short riddle story. This was for the kids to listen for two reasons: (1) it took their minds off their tests and, (2) because it was a fable that required them to guess the ending, it gave them something to think about with very little pressure attached. It was a five-minute reprieve from their testing.

— Sarah Schmaltz, Grade 4, Sunrise Elementary, Spokane, WA

Let's Look at Grandfather Bear

Once you know a story well enough to tell it, start thinking of all the ways you could use that tale. Each story can provide many curricular connections. Take a few moments to think over your tale and jot down possible ways you can use it to teach concepts in your curriculum. For example, let's take another look at "Grandfather Bear is Hungry." In addition to language arts uses, what are ways you could link the tale to your many areas of instruction?

Values Education: Discuss sharing, kindness, rewards for helping another, problem solving, and peaceful reconciliation. For example: chipmunk does not attack the bear tearing at his house, but asks what the problem is and solves it.

Math–Early Elementary: If Chipmunk could fit five nuts and five dried berries in his mouth at one time, how many things could he take to Grandfather Bear on one trip?

Math–Upper Elementary: If Grandfather Bear's stomach holds 175 cubic centimeters of nuts and berries and Chipmunk's mouth holds 13 cubic centimeters of nuts and berries, how many trips will it take to fill up the bear?

If Chipmunk's mouth can hold 10 dried berries and there are 500 dried berries in his home, how many trips will he make before he has given Grandfather Bear all of his berries?

Science: Talk about hibernation, habitats, animal foods, seasons, animal markings.

Health: Discuss foods, nutrition.

Social Studies: Find Siberia on a map. Find out about the *Even* people who tell this tale.

PE: Lots of deep knee bends or toe touches as chipmunk runs up and down…up and down. Plan a relay race during which chipmunks carry nuts in a spoon and run to feed Grandfather Bear.

Music: Create a musical motif for Grandfather Bear and one for Chipmunk. Retell the story with your musical accompaniment using rhythm instruments, Orff instruments, or whatever you have to make evocative sounds!

Art: Make bear and chipmunk masks. Create mosaics using seeds and nuts. Draw your favorite scene from the story.

Drama: Retell the story as story theatre by telling the tale and acting the parts at the same time. Make puppets or masks and use them to dramatize the story.

Once you know a story well, plan many ways to use it in your curriculum. If you take the time to jot down these curriculum connection ideas after you learn the story, you are more likely to remember to use the tale next year at just the right time!

Try a Tale!

"Pig and Bear Big Business" is an easy-to-share story with math connections. We provide two versions here—the first one is in simple English that is easy to tell, and the other is a pattern for telling the tale with a partner. "The Elephants and the Bees" also is fun to tell with a partner. It has connections to the study of forest fires, wildlife, and Thai culture.

Pig and Bear Big Business
A Folktale from Czechoslovakia

Pig and Bear decided to sell food.
Pig baked potatoes.
Bear fried doughnuts.
They took their food down to the market and set up shop.
"Baked potatoes! Baked potatoes! Five cents!" called Pig.
"Doughnuts! Doughnuts! Five cents!" called Bear.
Nobody bought anything.

Pretty soon Bear got hungry.
"Pig, how much are your potatoes?"
"Five cents."
"I have five cents! said Bear. I can buy one!"

Now Pig had sold one potato.
He decided to treat himself.
"How much are your doughnuts, Bear?"
"Five cents."
"Great! I've already earned five cents!"
So Pig bought a doughnut from Bear.

"Let's go sell some more."
"Baked potatoes! Baked potatoes! Five cents!" called Pig.
"Doughnuts! Doughnuts! Five cents!" called Bear.

"Lunch time."
Bear was hungry. He had sold one doughnut to Pig.
So he decided to have another baked potato. "I have five cents. I'll buy one."

It wasn't long before Pig began to feel hungry again.
He had five cents and he'd already made two sales this day.
So he treated himself to another doughnut.

They tried to sell some more.
"Baked potatoes! Baked potatoes! Five cents!" called Pig.
"Doughnuts! Doughnuts! Five cents!" called Bear.
Nobody bought anything.

By then it was almost teatime, and Bear was hungry again.
"Are your potatoes still five cents?"
So, of course, he had to buy another potato.

"Do you have any doughnuts left?" asked Pig.
Pig bought one.

"Baked potatoes! Baked potatoes! Five cents! called Pig.
"Doughnuts! Doughnuts! Five cents!" called Bear.
Still nobody bought anything.

Time to go home and Bear was hungry.
"Do you have any doughnuts left, Pig?"

"Just one. Five cents."
So Bear bought it and ate it.

Do you have any potatoes left, Bear?"
"Just one. Five cents."
"I'll buy it." Pig ate the last potato.

"Pig!" shouted Bear. "I sold EVERYTHING! I sold ALL my potatoes!"
"Me too!" hollered Pig. "I sold ALL my doughnuts.
"Let's count our money!"
They both checked their pockets.
Bear had the nickel he came with in the morning.
That was ALL the money they had!

They each sold everything but neither of them made any money?
How could that be?

Source: *Three Minute Tales* by Margaret Read MacDonald. (Atlanta: August House, 2004), p. 82-83. Retold from *Twelve Iron Sandals and Other Czechoslovak Tales* by Vit Horejs. (Englewood Cliffs, NJ: Prentice-Hall, 1985). *Motif B294 Animals in business relations.*

A Tandem Telling

Storyteller Gerald Fierst and Margaret have often told this story in tandem. It can be a really fun story to share in that way. Choose a student who takes direction well, and explain how you want him or her to respond. Assign the role of Pig and start telling the story. It helps to have a nickel to pass back and forth.

Pig and Bear Big Business
Tandem Version by Margaret Read MacDonald and Gerald Fierst

Bear: Pig and Bear decided to go into business.
Bear: "Bear made four doughnuts."
Pig: "Pig baked four potatoes."

[Pretend you are selling to audience…]
Bear: "Doughnuts! Doughnuts! Five cents apiece!"

Pig: "Baked Potatoes! Baked Potatoes! Five cents apiece!" *[Don't let anyone actually buy anything.]*

Bear: "I didn't sell anything."
Pig: "Me either."
Both: "Coffee time."
Bear asks Pig: "How much are your baked potatoes?"
Pig: "Five cents."
Bear: "I have five cents! I'll buy one!" *[You can use a real nickel. Pass it back and forth as you sell.]*
[Bear eats baked potato. Now pig is hungry.]
Pig: "How much are your doughnuts?"
Bear: "Five cents."
Pig: "I have five cents! I'll buy one!"

Both: "Let's go sell some more."

[Repeat sales pitch, they make no sales, one is hungry, asks how much, buys, eats, etc. Repeat at noon. At tea time. Snack at end of day before walking home. ALL sold! Excitement!]

Bear: "We sold EVERYTHING! Let's count our money!"
[Both look carefully in all pockets. Bear has one nickel, which he had when he came this morning. Make a big business of looking for the money and asking each other where it went.]

Pig and Bear ask audience:
"What happened? How is this possible? We sold EVERYTHING!"

Extending the Tale

- How much would Pig and Bear each have made if they had sold their foods to someone other than each other? What if they had charged ten cents per item? Twenty-five cents? If Pig had to buy raw potatoes for two cents each, how much profit could he make?

- Make baked potatoes and sell them. How much do you have to charge to make a profit? Add a cheese topping to your baked potatoes. What does that do to your profit?

The Elephants and the Bees
A Folktale from Thailand

Once a fire raged through the forest.
The elephants were terrified. They didn't know which way to go to escape.

Just then a cloud of bees buzzed over their heads.
"Bees! Bees! Help us! Fly high and tell us which way to go!"

"Sure, we'll help you, elephants!" The bees flew high.
They flew to the east. "Fire! Fire!"
They flew to the west. "Fire! Fire!"
They flew to the north. "Fire! Fire!"
They flew to the south. There was a river!

"Follow us, elephants!"
The bees led the way over the mountain and down to the river.
The elephants waded in until only their little noses were sticking out of the water.
Now, in those days elephants had tiny noses like a pig.
They stuck their little noses out of the water and they were safe.

Just then the smoke from the fire began to billow down the hill.
"Cough! Cough! Cough! Help us, elephants! The smoke will kill us!"
The bees were terrified of the smoke.
"Open your mouths, elephants. Open your mouths and let us fly inside!"

"Open our mouths?" asked the elephants.
"Open your mouths and let us fly inside. We will be safe there."

"Let bees get into our heads?
Well…the bees saved us. We should save them."
So the elephants opened their mouths and let the bees fly in.
"Bzzzzz…"
The elephants' heads were buzzing. They were going crazy.
"Bzzzz…"

The fire burned down the hill and leapt over the river, burned up the opposite hill, and burned away.

The smoke cleared.

And the elephants opened their mouths.

"Okay, Bees. You can come out now. The smoke is gone."

"Bzzzzzz…We like it in here. It's dark. It's comfy. We are going to stay here and make honey!"

"What? NOOO! The elephants' heads were buzzing. They were going crazy.

"We have got to get these bees out. How can we do it?

We can WASH them out."

The elephants all took big drinks of water and started to blow the water out their noses. *[To audience:]* Everyone take a big drink of water. Now BLOW it out your noses!

"Pra PREN! Pra PREN! Pra Pren!"

"It didn't work. Try it again"

"Pra PREN! Pra PREN! Pra Pren!"

"Try it again."

"Pra PREN! Pra PREN! Pra Pren!"

"Stop! Look what is happening to our noses!"

Every time the elephants blew water out, their noses got a little bit longer.

Now their noses were almost touching the ground.

"This isn't working! We have ruined our noses! What can we do?"

[To audience:] Is there anything that the bees are afraid of? *[Answer: smoke]*

"Smoke! We can SMOKE them out!"

The elephants built a big smoky fire.

[To audience:] Everyone take a big breath of smoke and hold your breath. *[Suck in breath.]*

"YES!" The bees couldn't stand the smoke! They flew out of the elephants' noses and flew away.

But the bees had liked living inside the elephants' heads.

So they found a hollow tree in the forest shaped just like the inside of an elephant's head. And they make their honey there.

Sometimes an elephant still gets the feeling that there are bees inside his head. When that happens, he sucks up water and squirts it out: "Pra PREN! Pra PREN! Pra Pren!"

If you see an elephant doing that, just tell him. "Don't worry, Mr. Elephant. The bees are all gone. The bees are all gone."

Source: Retold from *Shake-it-up Tales! Stories to Sing, Dance, Drum, and Act Out* by Margaret Read MacDonald (August House, 2000) and from *Thai Tales: Folktales of Thailand* by Supaporn Vathanaprida (Libraries Unlimited), 1994. *A2335.3 Origin and nature of animal's proboscis. B481.3 Helpful bees.*

About Telling the Story

Dr. Wajuppa Tossa, a Thai friend who tells this story, ends it by asking the children to pat the backs of their neighbors and say, "Don't worry, Mr. Elephant. The bees are all gone. The bees are all gone." It makes a very tender moment.

Extending the Tale

- Learn about beekeeping and the role of smoke in that profession.
- Learn about the uses of elephants in modern day Thailand.
- Read about some recent forest fires. How do they affect the wildlife?

Ready…Set…Tell!

Think about a particular curricular area of focus that you're working on with your students this year. Can you think of any stories you've heard before that would link well? Check out the folktale section of your school or community library. You will find these in the 398 and 398.2 Dewey Decimal sections. See if you can find a tale that will inspire your children to look at the content you are exploring in a different way. Choose one to tell this week!

Chapter 5: CULTURAL CONNECTIONS— Exploring Cultures Through Their Stories

The story, from "Rumpelstiltskin" to War and Peace, *is one of the basic tools invented by the human mind for the purpose of gaining understanding. There have been great societies that did not use the wheel, but there have been no societies that did not tell stories.*

— Ursula K. LeGuin

In our increasingly connected world it is critical that our students become globally minded. In an age of globalization and international interdependence, we need to understand one another in order to work productively together. Stories offer a perfect vehicle for broadening our perspective and looking at the world in new ways.

Stories carry within them the values and realities of the cultures in which they grew. As our children immerse themselves in these tales, they engage briefly with another culture. This is a way to travel among cultures without leaving our classrooms. By sharing the stories loved by children in Ghana or Vietnam or Brazil, we gain a slight peek into their worlds and a new perspective on our own lives.

Our libraries are full of world folktale collections and your librarian can help you find beautifully told tales from many cultures. The bibliographies in this book will also point the direction to tales from around the world that are easy to tell. Even if you cannot learn to *tell* them all, you can share them by reading aloud. With a bit of practice, though, you will find that telling the tale is easier than you thought, especially when it's a short folktale with repetitive patterns.

Building Empathy

Through stories children begin to empathize with those in other cultures. As we've mentioned before, when children enter the heart of the story, they tend to fall into a story-trance. Their eyes fix on those of the storyteller, their bodies are still, they are "in" the story. Once there, children can empathize completely with the tale's characters. Through this guided imagery, the audience can be led to feel with the tale's protagonists. They sense something of how it feels to be in the skin of another. For the space of the tale, the listener can enter another culture.

Children are often exposed to negative messages in the media about other countries that come into conflict with our own. By sharing folktales heard by the children in these countries, we help our children know that humanity is the same throughout the world. Stories can offer an antidote to fear and misunderstanding.

Sharing the Tale's Background

It's important when you share a folktale that you begin by mentioning where the story comes from. Tell about the country, region, or culture that told the story, and find it on a map or globe. If learning about a certain culture is the reason you are sharing a particular tale, you will want to go further and give your students more context. Some folktale collections will provide you with information about the tale and its teller. Some collections talk in-depth about how story is used in that culture, how it functions in that society. If that information is available, share it with your students.

Stories often carry references to certain cultural traditions that students may want to know more about. For example, when we tell "Ms. Cricket Gets Married" (p. 61), students sometimes ask, "Why did she ask the camel to put money in her sleeve?" We explain the tradition of a groom giving a dowry, presents or money, to a bride's family. Students listening to "Little Basket Weaver" (p. 103) might want to investigate Northwest Coast weaving traditions and look at pictures of cedar trees and cedar bark.

Honoring Your Students with Tales from Their Cultures

Students love hearing stories shared from their own cultures. The eyes of Japanese children light up when we tell "Momotaro," a story much loved in Japan. When we share the story "Five Threads," an Iraqi tale set at Ramadan, our Muslim students speak up: "We do that too! We fast at Ramadan." [Find "Five Threads" in *Celebrate the World: Twenty Tellable Folktales for Multicultural Festivals* by Margaret Read MacDonald (H.W. Wilson, 1994). "Momotaro" is found in Florence Sakade's *Peach Boy and Other Japanese Children's Favorite Stories* (Tuttle, 2008).]

For several years, Jen has worked in international schools with students from all over the world. She makes it a goal each year to find at least one story that represents each child's home culture. As soon as she says, "Here is a story from…," the student from that country beams, "That's *my* home!" Sometimes the class tracks these stories on a large world map. This visual reminder of the stories they have shared together sparks conversation throughout the year. "That story is just like Grandfather Bear because…" or "That character is acting like Koala because…"

Whether you have a diverse mix of students who come from many different countries or a more homogenous group with similar backgrounds, stories are an essential tool for helping students learn more about themselves and the world around them. Emily Style, the co-director of the National SEED (Seeking Educational Equity and Diversity) Project on Curriculum, talks about the need for curriculum to offer both mirrors and windows to students. ("Curriculum as Window and Mirror" in *Social Science Record*, Fall 1996, p. 35-42). Students need to see themselves in the curriculum and also need to have a way of learning that others are different from themselves in their customs and traditions. Stories are the perfect vehicle for this. They can function as a mirror to see their own culture reflected, or as a window through which they can view the cultures of others. When we find stories that honor each child's culture in our classroom, we are able to hold up a mirror for one child, while opening a window for the rest of the class.

By sharing folklore from their cultures of origin, my students can gain a greater appreciation and understanding of each other. They find common interests and beliefs that would not be explored if they had not studied and presented them in a story. Research shows students that get to know and trust each other will learn more effectively and gain greater knowledge.

— Janet Morgan, Grade 5, Bremerton WA.

Exploring Your Own Culture

Take a moment to think about stories you may have heard in your own childhood. Did your mother, grandfather, or aunt tell you stories? These tales frequently lie forgotten, but make great stories to share, once you recall them. Often they carry traces of your own cultural background within them. Margaret thought she had no folktales in her family until she told her father the first story she learned from a book. It was about a hound dog that chased a train. "Oh, that happened right here in North Vernon, Indiana!" her father informed her. "But it was about Old Joe Sutter who lives down by the railroad tracks." And he went on to tell her a wildly better version of the tale.

You really won't know if there are any stories lurking in your family unless you ask. By sharing stories from your own background, either folktales or true experiences, you offer a bit of your own cultural background to your students. If you would like to learn some folktales from the spot your ancestors arrived from, just ask your librarian to help you find some collections of folktales from Ireland, China, Iran, or wherever your roots lie.

Collecting Family Stories from Your Students

It is rewarding to spend some time helping your students collect stories from their families. We have had success doing a whole unit based around this project. Students interviewed family members and recorded or wrote down memories and stories. In an even easier activity, students brought in family photographs and heirlooms and told the stories behind these objects. The students can write down those background stories, preserving the stories for future generations! We put a large map on the wall and put pins in the places from which our students' ancestors had come. We also made family trees for each student and hung these on the wall. And to conclude our unit, we prepared to tell and dramatize episodes from their stories to share in a program for their families.

Here is a useful book to help you plan a family story unit: Linda Winston. *Keepsakes: Using Family Stories in Elementary Classrooms*. Portsmouth, N.J.: Heinemann, 1997. This book includes ideas for encouraging students to write and retell family stories. There are also suggestions for having the students' family members visit school to share stories; for conducting interviews with elders; and for the use of family recipes, photos, and family history.

Preserving Children's Cultures
Through Collecting Their Families' Folktales

Encouraging your students to share stories learned from their parents and to write these down or record them can help preserve these tales for future generations. Not many students will have families with living folktale traditions, but several might. It is worth suggesting that your students ask if their parents or grandparents know some stories they could share.

When we were traveling in Borneo a few years back, Yunis Rojin, the librarian who was taking us to libraries for our storytelling events suddenly said, "Oh! Your stories remind me of stories my grandmother told me when I was little." "What stories?" we wanted to know. Yunis began to tell us the most remarkable stories. We grabbed pencil and paper and Margaret noted the plots, while Nat jotted down the tunes for the songs that were an important part of Yunis' stories. As far as we know, these stories had never been written down before in any language—not Yunis's own Kadazan language, nor in the country's Malay language. Later Yunis remembered even more stories and instructed Margaret to bring her tape recorder on her next visit to Kota Kinabalu. Several of these stories were published in Margaret's book, *The Singing Top: Folktales of Malaysia, Singapore and Brunei* (Libraries Unlimited, .

2008), and Nat and Jen often tell them to their students. If we hadn't taken the time to stop and listen, those stories might have been lost for all time.

We often hear it said that traditional storytelling is dead. Well, not quite yet—and if *you* will start sharing stories and getting your students to tell stories—maybe it never will be. Margaret was able to solicit over one hundred articles about contemporary traditional storytelling around the world for her *Traditional Storytelling Today* (Fitzroy-Dearborn, 1999). And if you would like to read about the excitement traditional tellers feel about sharing their art, take a look at her *Ten Traditional Tellers* (University of Illinois Press, 2006). Since there is less opportunity for sharing stories now, people assume no one remembers any of the old folktales. But if we ask, sometimes amazing stories emerge. You and your students may be able to discover some delightful cultural treasures, just by asking your elders. The stories are out there, but we need to shake the tree, catch the fruit—and share it around.

Cross-Cultural Study of One Tale

Folktales are passed from culture to culture. They travel literally around the world, and they change slightly with each telling. So, you will find the same story told in Africa, Asia, Latin America, Europe. All the versions will have recognizably similar motifs, but each will be shaded by the culture in which it was nurtured.

Students enjoy hearing many versions of the same tale. This provides a good opportunity to work on text comparisons. How are the tales the same? How are they different? What specific embroideries does each culture use to make the story its own? After studying several versions of Cinderella, Beauty and the Beast, or other such universal tale types, the students will be ready to write their own adaptation. A folktale pattern makes a perfect starting point for student writing.

You can find variants of tales by consulting motif and type indexes. You can look up stories by subject or title in *The Storyteller's Sourcebook: A Subject, Title, and Motif-Index of Folk-Literature for Children* by Margaret Read MacDonald (Gale Research, 1982) and in *The Storyteller's Sourcebook: A Subject, Title, and Motif-Index of Folk-Literature for Children 1983–1999* by Margaret Read MacDonald and Brian L. Sturm. (Gale Research, 2001). There you will find, for just one example, several pages of descriptions of Cinderella variants from around the world along with their sources.

For collections with about thirty folktale variants of one tale type see the Oryx Folktales of the World Series, which includes *Cinderella* by Judy Sierra (Oryx, 1991), *Beauties and Beasts* by Betsy Hearne (Oryx, 1993), *Tom Thumb* by Margaret Read MacDonald (Oryx, 1993), and a *Knock at the Door* by George Shannon, with variants on tales about the wolf and the seven little kids (Oryx, 1992).

Connecting Students to World Folk Literature

Many of our students have no background in the standard nursery tales that form cultural references in our literature. They may know "Three Little Pigs," "Little Red Hen," and others only as parodies seen on TV or in fractured-folktale picture books. Sharing these stories with kindergarten and primary students gives the children a background in the folktale traditions that they will see referenced in different formats.

With older students, use storytelling to introduce mythology and epic heroes. The Greek and Roman myths are action-packed and make great stories to tell. Select episodes from the adventures of King Arthur, or connect your students to world literature through sharing tales from the Indian Ramayana, or stories of the Chinese Monkey King, Sun Wu Kung.

Over half of my class was born in another country and speaks another language at home. I have found they have limited background of American and other cultural folktales. So, taking the chance to retell the classic tales to my students is a wonderful opportunity I can't pass up.

— Kelly McCarty, Cedar Valley Community School, Lynwood, WA.

Storytelling Techniques from Other Cultures

Various ways of sharing story are employed throughout the world. In some traditions in India, the teller hangs up a fabric with painted pictures of scenes from the story and refers to them as the story is told. The Yupik and other Alaskan groups have sometimes told stories while drawing in the snow with knives, a manner of telling known as story knifing. Anne Pellowski's books *The Story Vine* (MacMillan, 1984) and *The Family Storytelling Handbook* (MacMillan, 1987) show many ways in which story has been shared around the world through paper cutting, handkerchief folding, drawing, string figures, object manipulation, and other techniques. You or your students may enjoy incorporating these folk traditions into your own telling.

In Japan, traveling candy vendors carried wooden *kamishibai* boxes on their bicycles. Setting picture cards up in these wooden frames, they would tell a story, showing illustrations from the tale, then sell candy to the gathering. This is a very gentle way for beginners to start sharing story. Pictures of the story are made and the story text is written on the back of the picture card which was just shown. The teller holds the picture and shares the story using the written text as a prompt. This can be a fun story-learning activity for your students. To learn more about this technique or to purchase imported Japanese *kamishibai* story cards see www.kamishibai.com.

Should I Tell Stories of Cultures Other than My Own?

For thousands of years stories have traveled around the world, passed from culture to culture. Each teller takes the story, adapts it, and makes it live in the new culture into which it has now entered. Though there is sometimes talk now of cultures and tellers "owning" their stories, the fact is that once a story is spoken it cannot be taken back. It lodges in the mind of the listener and is carried away. Stories have a way of ensuring their own survival. They find a host, jump aboard, and travel.

If you are living in an area in which certain ethnic tellers object to the use of their stories, by all means, respect their needs. Australian Aboriginal and Native American groups, for example, sometimes establish ownership over certain tales. The tales might belong to tribes, clans, families, or individuals. These are considered cultural possessions and are not free for others to tell. Some tales are considered sacred and are not for use outside the culture group. Some stories are only meant to be told in a particular season or for a certain occasion.

Most of the world's peoples, though, have no restrictions on their stories and are pleased to have them shared by others. It gives people a sense of pride in their own culture to know that others love their stories, too. When adapting a story from a culture with which you are unfamiliar, do all you can to find out about the use of story in that culture. Try to frame your telling in a way to help your students appreciate the culture from which the story comes.

Researching Your Tale's Background

To find more information you can share about your tale, check any notes in the back of the collection and read the jacket flap information. Consult motif-indexes, such as *The Storyteller's Sourcebook* (Gale Research, 1982 and 2001), to see if there are other variants of the story. Look for books about storytelling traditions in this culture. You can search online, find a member of the culture who can help you learn more about the tale's background, and ask your librarian for help.

For two books that provide deep insight into a particular culture's storytelling traditions see: *The Magic Orange Tree and Other Haitian Folktales* by Diane Wolkstein (Schocken, 1997) and *Why Leopard Has Spots: Dan Stories from Liberia* by Won-Ldy Paye and Margaret H. Lippert (Fulcrum, 1999).

Let's Look at Grandfather Bear

So let's visit Grandfather Bear again. You can have a discussion with your class about why the Even people would tell a story like this. The Even (pronounced e as in "ever") are a reindeer herding people of Siberia. You can search online for information about "Even" and "Evens." Find Siberia on a map and discuss the climate there.

Try a Tale!

The stories below were told by tellers who have two very different approaches to story sharing. Vi **taq š blu** Hilbert was an Upper Skagit elder from the NW Coast of the United States. Pauline McLeod was an Australian Aboriginal teller of the Wiradjuri people. Each came from a culture that considers folktales to be owned objects. Stories are not available for just anyone to share. Vi has selected tales which she feels need to be shared beyond her own Lushootseed-speaking culture and published them as *Haboo: Native American Stories from Puget Sound* (University of Washington, 1985). Pauline has talked with elders in her culture and received permission to share certain stories for educational purposes. These she taught in workshops and published.

However, these two tellers suggest totally different ways to use the stories. Vi says one should never ask the audience about the meaning of the story. One should respect each individual and let them draw their own conclusions from the story they have just been given. On the other hand, during a Sydney workshop, Pauline taught that a story should have 18 morals! She suggested that we ask the children to think of morals they had learned from the story.

When we tell these stories we respect the wishes of both tellers. We never ask an audience what they have learned from one of Vi's stories. But we do follow "How Kangaroo Got Her Pouch" by asking the listeners to come up with 18 things they learned from listening. These can be morals or bits of information about nature and Australia—any new insight gained from hearing the story.

Little Basket Weaver
A Klickitat Folktale

Retold with permission of Upper Skagit elder, Vi **taq š blu** Hilbert.

Sometimes it was hard for this girl to think.
It was hard for her to figure things out.
The other girls wouldn't play with her, because she couldn't understand their games.

One day the girl was sitting all by herself under the Cedar Tree.
The Cedar Tree bent over. "Girl, why are you by yourself?
Why aren't you playing with the other children?"
"They don't like to play with me," said the girl. "I can't understand their games."

"That's too bad," said the tree.
"I have an idea. Would you like to learn how to make a cedar basket?"

"I wouldn't be able to do that," said the girl. "It would be too hard."
"But I could teach you," said the tree.

"No. It's hard for me to understand things."

"Well, girl…could you *try*?"

"I could try."

"Good!" said the tree. "Good!"
And the tree told her just what to do.
Tree told Girl where to dig special roots and how to prepare them.
Tree told her how to take bark from the Cedar Tree and prepare it.

And Tree told her how to weave.
She wove and she wove and…she wove a little cedar basket.

"Yes!" said the Cedar Tree. "That's FINE!"
"Now take your basket to the stream and bring me water."

Girl took the basket to the stream and dipped it. It was very light.
She brought the basket back and showed it to the tree.
The basket was empty. The water had all run out.
"Girl, you didn't weave it tight enough. Can you do it again?"

"Again? I guess so." So, Girl began again.
She gathered roots and treated them.

She took bark from the cedar tree and prepared it.
And she wove. This time she wove more tightly.
She wove…and she wove…and…she wove a little cedar basket.

She showed it to the tree.
"Well, take the basket to the stream and bring water."

The girl took the basket to the stream. She dipped it. It was heavier this time.
She brought it back to the Cedar Tree.
It was half full of water.
"Girl, this is better. But it is not good enough.
Can you do it again?"
"Do it again? I guess so."

So, the Girl began again.
She gathered more roots and treated them.
She took more bark from the Cedar Tree and prepared it.
And she began to weave again.
This time she wove very carefully. She wove very tightly.
And she wove…and she wove…

The Cedar Tree saw how well she was weaving this time.
"Why don't you weave a design into the top of your basket?" asked the Cedar Tree.
"You could copy my branches."
Tree held out a drooping branch. "Put that pattern in."
"I like that!" So, Girl copied the Cedar Tree's branches.
She made a little zigzag pattern all around the top of her basket.

And she wove…and she wove…and she wove a little cedar basket.

She showed it to the tree.
"It is beautiful, Girl!" said Cedar Tree. "That is a beautiful cedar basket!"
"Well…bring me water."

Girl took her basket to the stream and dipped it.
It felt very heavy this time.
She carried it back to the Cedar Tree.
She held it up.
The basket was FULL of water.
"Girl you have done it! You have made a perfect cedar basket!"

"Now, Girl…now what should you do?"

"I think…I should weave MORE baskets.
And give them to all the elders in my tribe."

"Yes," said the Cedar Tree. "That is a fine idea!
Girl, is there anything else you should do…
Now that you know how to weave cedar baskets?"

"I think…I should teach all the girls and all the women how to make cedar baskets."

"Yes, Girl. That is exactly what you should do."

And so today—because of that one girl—
All the girls and all the women of the Klickitat people
Know how to weave beautiful cedar baskets.

Source: The text for this story was sent to Margaret by Lushootseed teller, Vi taq š blu Hilbert and we also heard her tell it many times. Vi told mostly stories of her own Upper Skagit people, but this Klickitat story spoke to her. She felt it was important that this story be shared.

About Telling the Story

Margaret holds her left hand as if it is her basket and moves her right index finger in and out among her left fingers as if weaving. Then she cups both hands together as if it is a basket. The first time she holds her fingers slightly apart, as if water could run out.

Extending the Tale

- Find pictures of cedar trees, cedar root baskets and cedar bark baskets online.

- Research the Klickitat people.

- Follow this story with a weaving project. Simple patterns for weaving a paper basket can be found online by searching for "paper basket craft."

Old Man Wombat
A Wiradjuri Aboriginal Folktale from New South Wales, Australia

Retold with permission of Pauline McLeod, Wiradjuri Aboriginal teller from Sydney, Australia.

Mother Kangaroo and her little Joey were hopping along.
Mother Kangaroo took big kangaroo hops.
Her baby Joey just took little hops.

They met Old Man Wombat.
He could not see well. He was very slow.

"Mother Kangaroo, is that you?" asked Old Man Wombat.
"Is that your little Joey?"
[Pause after each of Old Man Wombat's statements, so the Old Man Wombat actor can repeat it after you.]
"Mother Kangaroo, I am lost. I can't find my home."

"I know where your home is," said Mother Kangaroo. "I will take you there.
But my little Joey can't keep up. I will leave him by the gum tree.

[Settle Joey in a chair.]

"Joey, you must wait here. Mother will come back.
I have to help Old Man Wombat."

[Lead Old Man Wombat around the room. Make a large circle during the story so you can arrive back at the front of the room when he finds his home.]

"Walk this way, Old Man Wombat…walk this way….
Walk this way, Old Man Wombat…walk this way…."

[Continue for quite a while. You might encourage your audience to repeat this with you as you go.]

"Wait here Old man Wombat. This is taking a long time.
I have to go back and see if my Joey is okay."

HOP HOP HOP HOP HOP
[Hop back the way you came until you reach Joey.]
"Good boy, Joey! You are waiting for Mamma.
I have to help Old Man Wombat. He is very old. He needs our help. I will come back."

HOP HOP HOP HOP
[Return to Old Man Wombat.]

"Joey is okay, Old Man Wombat. We can go now."

"Walk this way, Old Man Wombat…walk this way…
Walk this way, Old Man Wombat…walk this way…"

"Old Man Wombat, I should go back and check on my little Joey. Wait here."

HOP HOP HOP HOP HOP

"Good boy, Joey! You are very patient waiting for Mamma.
Old Man Wombat is very slow. He needs help. I will come back soon."

HOP HOP HOP HOP HOP

"We can go now, Old Man Wombat.
Walk this way, Old Man Wombat…walk this way…
Walk this way, Old Man Wombat…walk this way…
"Old Man Wombat, I think this is your home."

Old Man Wombat went into his hole.
He turned around three times.

He said, "This is my home!"
[As teller, you say "He said, 'This is my home!'" and indicate to Old Man Wombat that he should say that. He then repeats everything you suggest.]

Old Man Wombat said: "Mother Kangaroo, I want to thank you.
I see you have trouble taking care of your little Joey."

"Yes, I do."

Old Man Wombat said: "Would you like a pouch to carry him?"

"Could you do that?"

Old Man Wombat said: "I can make a magic!"
[Look expectantly at Old Man Wombat. He will usually wave a pretend wand and say "Abracadabra!" or something like that. Jump when he zaps you.]

"Thank you, Old Man Wombat! THANK YOU!"

HOP HOP HOP HOP HOP

"Joey! See what we have! Jump in!"
[Have Joey pretend to jump in your pouch. Hold onto him from behind and…]

HOP HOP HOP HOP HOP

And that is how Mother Kangaroo got her pouch.

Source: This story is retold from a tale taught to Margaret by Wiradjuri Aboriginal teller, Pauline McLeod, during a workshop in Sydney, Australia. Pauline later wrote down a version of the story, which appears in *Gaddi Mirrabooka: Australian Aboriginal Tales from the Dreaming*, retold by Pauline E. McLeod, Francis Firebrace Jones, and June E. Barker, edited by Helen F. McKay (Libraries Unlimited, 2001). This is a Wiradjuri story from New South Wales. Old Man Wombat was, in fact, Biamee, the Creator Spirit. You could include that fact in the story. It explains why Old Man Wombat could make a magic pouch.

Extending the Tale

- We suggest telling the story as story-theater. Choose audience members to act the parts of Old Man Wombat and Baby Joey. You act the part of Mother Kangaroo. Arrange a chair for Joey to sit in under the gum tree. Your chosen actors will take their direction from your words, providing the actions as you describe them.

- Let children suggest the 18 lessons that can be found in this story. Any answer is correct. Count them up until you elicit 18. For example, they might say: Mind your mother. Take care of old people. Look after your children. Wombats live in holes.

- Find pictures of Wombats online.

- Share picture books, such as *Diary of a Wombat* by Jackie French, illustrated by Bruce Whatley (Sandpiper, 2009) and *Wombat Goes Walkabout* by Michael Morpurgo, illustrated by Christian Birmingham (Harper Collins, 2000).

- Research the Wiradjuri.

- For younger children, play at hopping like kangaroos. Use clacking sticks to set the beat. Children stand in a circle and hop around. Demonstrate how to take big, slow hops for Father Kangaroo, medium hops for Mother Kangaroo and tiny, rapid hops for Baby Kangaroo. Your clacking tells the children which kind of hops to take. Later, let the children take turns clacking the sticks to direct the hopping.

Ready...Set...Tell!

Take a moment to think about the students in your classroom. What cultures are represented in your room? Can you think of stories from each of those cultures? Visit your school library or local library and find a tale that you could share to honor each child in your class at some point during the year.

Chapter 6: CREATIVITY— Creating Divergent Thinkers and Extending Stories with the Arts

Left unhampered, a child begins very young to put into everyday life a series of masterpieces of creative thinking and doing. It is as if he were always saying: "This I like. This I will make—sing—play—be."

— Ruth Sawyer, *The Way of the Storyteller*

Creativity is at the heart of the human experience. We want our students to be able to generate ideas and find new ways to contribute to our rapidly changing society. Many current educational thinkers are proposing that creativity and original thinking are the most important skills we need to be developing in our twenty-first-century students. The prominent educationalist Sir Ken Robinson put it this way in his famous February 2006 TED talk:

"Creativity now is as important in education as literacy and we should treat it with the same status."

(www.ted.com/talks/ken_robinson_says_schools_kill_creativity.html)

Once again, stories come to the rescue! The skills that our children need for the future can be cultivated through this most important tool from our past. Storytelling provides a perfect pathway for students to explore their imaginations and foster their own creativity.

Divergent Thinking

We love to tell stories that have improvisational slots where we can incorporate ideas from students. These allow the children to chime in with their own suggestions for the story. When sharing "Little Crab with the Magic Eyes" (found at the end of this chapter), we always stop to take several ideas for the kinds of sea creatures that Little Crab can see under the water when he makes his eyes go sailing. "Little Crab looked down into the water and he saw…" Here we pause to take suggestions from the audience, " Yes! That's right! He saw a purple starfish! What else did he see? Of course! A shimmering jellyfish!" We can incorporate a quick brainstorming activity in the middle of any story.

Many of the tales in this book lend themselves well to improvisation. In telling "The Squeaky Door" (p. 158), you could let the children suggest what animal the grandmother brought into the bed next and tell you what noise they made when they cried. The story structure is clear, but the actual animals included could vary as long as something heavy comes in last and breaks the bed. In "The Elephants and the Bees" (p. 92), we often have the children suggest ways to get rid of the bees.

The Little Crab story features a scary Oonka Loonka Fish. Students are always mesmerized by the idea of an Oonka Loonka Fish. "But, what does it *look* like?" We are always asked. "What do *you* think an Oonka Loonka Fish looks like?" we reply. We have students draw or paint a picture of this imaginary Oonka Loonka Fish and then talk about the visual characteristics they chose to give their sea creature. We make a gallery of Oonka Loonka Fish in the classroom to showcase how we each create our very own unique images in our minds.

Another extension we often use to help students develop descriptive language is a "barrier activity" in which a visual barrier is set up between two students and each tries to describe the Oonka Loonka Fish they have drawn, while a partner listens carefully and tries to follow the oral directions in order to draw the same fish.

Developing Imaginative Stories from Scratch

Tellers who are comfortable with improvisation often let the children direct the story as they tell, developing connecting tissue to keep the tale whole as they go along. The teller Floating Eagle Feather created the feeling that the children were in fact making up a story by telling a story with a set pattern but asking the children to suggest details. "Where shall we travel?" "How shall we travel?" He then told the story of the trip, pausing to ask, "What monster did we meet? Of course, he had a clear structure of the story in his mind before he began—travel, meet monster, defeat monster, return home. He just let the children provide the details. After this story-creating experience, several five year olds were empowered to come to the front and tell their *own* made-up story to the group.

Storytelling Games

Storytelling games are a perfect way to encourage divergent thinking in your classroom. Students strengthen their ability to generate new ideas, work collaboratively, and develop flexible thinking through these games. Here are two quick theater improvisation games that you can play with your students to foster creativity.

"YES, AND…"

This is a game that is perfect to use with students to generate stories. The idea is that with a partner or on a team, one person starts the story and the next person says, "YES, AND…" and then moves the story forward. For example,

Student 1: There was a little girl named Annie who was walking down the beach.

Student 2: YES, AND she was looking for treasures. She found a beautiful shell.

Student 3: YES, AND when Annie put the shell up to her ear she could hear a voice…

With younger students this works best in small groups where everyone can have multiple turns to add input to the story. For older students, it could be a whole-class activity and more guidelines can be added to include particular story elements: conflict, a resolution, character details, a detailed orientation, etc. Saying, "YES, AND" requires students to acknowledge the thinking that has gone before them. It helps them tune into what others are contributing to the story as it is being developed. Most importantly, it helps them to be open to the new direction that the story will take and to learn to be flexible in how they carry story forward.

Story, Story, Drop

Older students enjoy playing an extension of "YES, AND" called "Story, Story, Drop." In this competitive game, a teacher or student is the conductor of the story. The conductor points to one student to begin the story. After a few moments, the conductor points to another student to carry on the story. Students must pick up the story line at the exact place where it left off, without any "ums" or "ahs" or repeating what has just been said. If the story doesn't flow, the student storyteller who "drops" the story "drops" to the floor and the conductor points to someone else to carry on. After students have played this for a while and have gotten really good, the conductor can be ruthless, switching storytellers mid-sentence or even mid-word, until there is one storyteller left standing to finish the story.

Storytelling in the Arts

Storytelling can inspire your students to show their creativity through the arts. Once inside a tale, students connect to the story on many different levels. When students have experienced the themes and emotions of a tale while listening to a told story, they can draw upon those memories to express themselves creatively. Responding to a story artistically serves a reverse purpose as well: it lodges the story even more securely in a student's mind. The story that is carried home in the form of a picture, clay pot, or a basket will be remembered longer. A tale that is sung, danced, or acted out, will sink down into the bones of the student and linger. And so, the story evolves, creating a joyful, holistic experience.

All folktales lend themselves readily to interpretation through dramatic play, puppetry, mask making, painting, music, movement, or any other artistic expression. Here are some of the ways teachers have enjoyed connecting storytelling to their Arts curricula.

Drama

A logical extension for any storytelling experience is to act out the story in multiple ways. We tell our story first, then ask, "Would you like to *play* the story?" We let the children choose their parts. If three want to be the dog, we put three dogs in the bed with the little boy in "Squeaky Door." Any character can be acted by several children, rather than depriving someone of the joy of being their favorite character. Or we can always add in extra characters. In "Ms. Mouse Needs a Friend" (p. 42) we let students think of other animals that might come to help her and decide what fault she will find with each.

For the youngest children, we don't expect them to speak parts in these re-enactments. We just tell the story and let the children move through it devising their own actions. For older children, we tell the story, stopping for each actor to speak for his character. And of course, those who have worked with the story several times can just act and speak their lines for the whole story with no guidance from you.

Group dramatization is a quick way to involve the entire class in acting out a story. Using stories with two main characters, we divide the class into halves and assign one role to each half. We act the story out together. For example, in "Grandfather Bear" all the bears forage for food and growl "I am so hungry," then all the chipmunks scurry down to fill their cheeks with food. A little playfulness is all you need to let these stories loose in your classroom.

Stories provide an excellent base for dramatic productions. There are no scripts to read or memorize. Knowledge of the story line will allow your students to improvise their dialogue. Add a few simple costume elements or props and—voila! You have a parent-night performance.

Art

There are so many ways to expand a story through art activities…mask making, puppets, drawing scenes from the story, murals. Here are some ways art teachers have connected story directly with their art curriculum.

The Palestinian folktale *Tunjur Tunjur! Tunjur* by Margaret Read MacDonald, illustrated by Alik Arzoumanian (Marshall Cavendish, 2006) was used by Jessica Holloway to inspire her fifth-grade students before an art project.

In the story, a pot steals things that are placed in her. She is rewarded for her theft by being filled with goat dung. We created ceramic face-jugs inspired by Appalachian Face Jugs. Students explored sketching facial expressions and then created a pot expression. When we exhibited the pots in the library, students created tags as a culminating activity to tell the viewer what their pot's mouth is full of, just like the story. The expressiveness of the story really helped my students stretch their imaginations to think about which materials in a mouth would result in which face.

— Jessica Holloway, Art Teacher, Clyde Hill Elementary, Bellevue, WA

Jessica also told her students the Klickitat Native American tale of "Little Basket Weaver" (p. 103) to inspire a basket weaving unit. She used the tale to encourage them to try again and again and approach their work with a patient and forgiving attitude.

I feel that my storytelling is a great community building opportunity. My storytelling has given my six hundred students the chance to see another creative, more entertaining, side of me and they are amazing listeners when a story is being told. My fellow teachers have been impressed with my efforts.

— Jessica Holloway, Art Teacher, Clyde Hill Elementary, Bellevue, WA

Art teacher Megan Garner used the story of Medusa to inspire a unit:

When I used the story "Medusa" to introduce my lesson on line and pattern, the students were hooked from the start. I can imagine telling them simply that we were going to make Medusa heads and snakes. This would have gotten a pretty bland response. I recall during the telling that the moment I described the transformation to a snake head, the kids' heads shot up. There was a level of investment about what was going to happen that I don't always see when I introduce something new.

— Megan Garner, Interlake High School and Chinook Middle School, Bellevue, WA

Music

In many cultures, music and story are intertwined. Tales may contain singing refrains—sometimes even dancing is included in the telling. Adding musical effects to any tale can expand the experience.

Second-grade teacher Robin Earwood makes good use of the Ugandan singing tale "Ttimba" to teach African drumming patterns to his students. In the tale Lizard carries off the drum of Ttimba the Python without permission. Both Python and Lizard do a lot of drumming. There are great places for listeners to drum along—in a guided pattern, as Robin did—or just in a random banging. It will be fun either way. Find the story in *Songs and Stories from Uganda* by W. Moses Serwadda (Crowell, 1974).

> I tell "Ttimba" to my second graders every year. They **LOVE** it!! I am even going to tell that story during our city-wide annual "Celebrate the Arts Day" we have every year in Roswell in May.
>
> — Robin Earwood, Grade 2 Performing Arts Educator, Creative Learning Center, Roswell, New Mexico.

In this book, you will find musical motifs in the stories of "Mabela the Clever" (p. 25) and "Mona Monissima!" (p. 123). And you can sing the jig in "The Teeny Weeny Bop" (p. 64), if you like. You don't need to have any musical talent to use song in a story. Just sing the tune any way you want. These are folktales. Folktales change every time they are told—and the folksongs within them change, too! Any way you want to sing is just fine. Actually, the less professional your singing sounds, the more likely your audience will feel free to chime in along with you. If you really, really can't bring yourself to sing, then just chant the refrains. That works fine too, and still adds a bit of rhythm and musicality to the story.

Here is a short list of singing and dancing stories you might have fun with:

"Nsangi" in *Songs and Stories from Uganda* by W. Moses Serwadda (New York: Crowell, 1974). A singing gorilla tricks Nsangi, but her mother sings to rescue her daughter from the ten gorillas.

Conejito: A Folktale from Panama by Margaret Read MacDonald, illus. by Geraldo Valerio (Atlanta: August House, 2006). A singing rabbit is threatened by fox, tiger, and lion. The rabbit rolls down a hill and escapes with the aid of a dancing auntie. Includes some Spanish refrains.

Old Woman and Her Pig: An Appalachian Folktale by Margaret Read MacDonald, illus. by John Kanzler (New York: Harper Collins, 2007). An old woman can't get home because her pig won't cross a bridge. She sings a plaintive song, but along come a dog, rat, and cat creating a chain—cat scares rat bites dog barks at pig. They all go singing home.

Lizard's Song by George Shannon, illus. by Jose Aruego and Ariane Dewey, (New York: Harper *Trophy*, 1992). Lizard is threatened because of his song. (also available in Spanish as: *La Canción del Lagarto*, Greenwillow, 1994).

"Toad and Horse" in *The Magic Orange Tree and Other Haitian Folktales* by Diane Wolkstein, (New York: Schocken, 1997). Racing along, Toad and horse each sing their song as they reach the mileposts.

Pickin' Peas by Margaret Read MacDonald, illus. by Pat Cummins (New York: Harper Collins, 1998). Rabbit sings happily as he eats up Little Girl's peas.

Abiyoyo by Pete Seeger, illus. by Michael Hayes (New York: Simon & Schuster, 2001). Singing brings about the demise of a nasty giant.

The First Music, by Dylan Pritchett, Illustrated by Erin Bennett (Atlanta: August House, 2006). The jungle animals join together to create the music of nature. Fun filled story with refrains for active audience participation.

Dance

Many stories that are told in African and Caribbean cultures actually have dances within the stories. The entire audience might jump up and dance at certain points during the storytelling. Some of these tales have been retold in English language versions. They are great fun for your students and a wonderful way to incorporate movement, music, and language in one exciting event!

Here are a few of our favorite dancing tales and don't forget to dance when you tell "Mona Monissima" found at the end of this chapter.

"Bouki Dances the Kokioko" in *The Magic Orange Tree and Other Haitian Folktales* by Diane Wolkstein (New York: Schocken, 1997), p. 79-86. Ti Malice teaches slow-moving Bouki how to sing and dance to win the king's dance contest.

"Owl" in *The Magic Orange Tree and Other Haitian Folktales* by Diane Wolkstein (New York: Schocken, 1997) p. 29-36. Owl knows he is ugly, still the girl likes him. But at the dance, tragedy strikes.

Dance Away by George Shannon, illus. by Jose Aruego and Ariane Dewey (New York: Greenwillow, 1991). The animals dance away from Fox.

"Poule and Roach" in *Celebrate the World: Twenty Tellable Folktales for Multicultural Festivals* by Margaret Read MacDonald (New York: H.W. Wilson, 1994), p. 32-31. Cockroach and his buddies dance when the hen goes off to work.

"Kanji-Jo, the Nestlings" in *Tuck-Me-In Tales: Bedtime Stories from Around the World* by Margaret Read MacDonald (Atlanta: August House, 1996). Five little chicks sing their lost mother's song, and dance as they search for her.

Collections with Musical Tales

Shake-it-up Tales: Stories to Sing, Dance, Drum, and Act-Out by Margaret Read MacDonald (Atlanta: August House, 2000).

The Singing Sack: 28 Song-Stories from Around the World by Helen East. (London: A&C Black, 1989).

Let's Look at Grandfather Bear

Let's look at *Grandfather Bear* again through the lens of Creativity and the Arts. Here are a few ideas to get you started:

Act it Out: Our first impulse with any story is to have the children act out the story. Instruct the students to trade off being Grandfather Bear and Chipmunk.

Improvise: What would happen if Grandfather Bear were to meet a different animal in the woods? Would it change the story if he met a bird or a rabbit? Try acting out these different scenarios to see where the story leads!

Music: We love to link songs to stories. Matthew Jolly, a teacher from Australia, taught us a "Hungry" song that works well with this tale: "I'm so hungry, so hungry, so very, very hungry! I'm so hungry, so hungry, so very, very hungry! I want something I can munch, I want something I can crunch, I haven't had my lunch, I'm so hungry! I'm so hungry, so hungry, so hungry!" The song was originally from the Australian children's television program Play School. You can search for the tune on-line. Children love moving around like Grandfather Bear singing the hungry song.

Make up your own song! Have students work as partners to make up a theme song for Grandfather Bear or Chipmunk. How would their songs be different?

Visual Arts: Paint a picture of Grandfather Bear and Chipmunk. Make a wood-print show-ing Chipmunk's stripes. Create a seed mosaic with nuts and berries to express the story.

Dance: How would Grandfather Bear dance? What about chipmunk? What music would they each like to dance to? Create a dance for Grandfather Bear and one for Chipmunk, then split the class in two and have a dance-off between the chipmunks and the bears.

Try a Tale!

While all tales offer great possibilities to expand our creativity, some are especially fun to play with. We love the art and drama possibilities in "Little Crab with the Magic Eyes." And it is a delight to jump up and sing and dance with the Cuban tale of "Mona Monissima."

Little Crab with the Magic Eyes
A Tale from the Taulipang People of Brazil and British Guyana

There once was a little crab with *magic eyes*.
Little Crab could make his eyes POP out of his head
And go *sailing* out over the ocean!

He would sit by the shore and call
    "Little Eyes…Little Eyes…
    Sail OUT…over the deep blue sea."

Little Crab's eyes would POP out of his head and SAIL out over the deep blue sea!
His eyes would look far down into the water.
They would see blue fish—yellow fish—red fish.
They could see green seaweed.
They could see purple starfish!

    "Little Eyes…Little Eyes…
    Sail BACK over the deep blue sea!"

Little Crab's eyes would SAIL back
And POP into his head again.
This was a *lot* of fun!

One day Jaguar came by.

"What are you doing, Little Crab?"
"I'm playing my magic eye-sailing game!
I can make my eyes sail out over the deep blue sea and sail back again!"

"Little Crab, could you make *my* eyes go sailing?"

"I could. But it is *too* dangerous. Out in the deep blue sea lives an Oonka-Loonka Fish! The Oonka-Loonka Fish might come up and swallow your eyes!"

"I'm not afraid of any old Oonka-Loonka Fish," said Jaguar.
"You make my eyes go SAILING.
You make my eyes go SAILING or you'll be SORRY!"

Ok...ok..." Little Crab began to chant.
"Jaguar's eyes...Jaguar's eyes...
Sail OUT...over the deep blue sea!

Jaguar's eyes POPPED out of his head and SAILED out over the deep blue sea.
Jaguar's eyes looked down.
They could see blue fish—yellow fish—red fish.
They could see green seaweed.
They could see purple starfish!

"Ooohhh! I like it! I like it!" cried Jaguar.

Then Little Crab called.

"Jaguar's eyes...Jaguar's eyes...
Sail BACK...over the deep blue sea."

And Jaguar's eyes sailed BACK and POPPED into his head again.

"Do it *again*!" Do it *again*!" said Jaguar.
"Make my eyes go sailing!"

"No." said Little Crab. "It is *too* dangerous:

The Oonka-Loonka Fish might come up and swallow your eyes."

"I'm not afraid of any old FISH!"
"Do it again…or you'll be SORRY!"

"Ok. Just one more time."

"Jaguar's eyes…Jaguar's eyes…
Sail OUT…over the deep blue sea!"

Jaguar's eyes POPPED out of his head and SAILED out over the deep blue sea.

"Jaguar's eyes…Jaguar's eyes…
Sail BACK…over the deep blue sea!"

But just then the Oonka-Loonka Fish came up and SWALLOWED Jaguar's eyes!

"Little Crab it all went dark! Bring back my eyes!"

"It is TOO LATE!" said Little Crab. "The Oonka-Loonka Fish has swallowed your eyes."

Jaguar began to moan and groan. But just then, along came Vulture.

"Jaguar, why are you moaning and groaning?"

"Little Crab made my eyes go sailing and now he won't bring them back!"

"I can bring you some new eyes. Wait right here."

Vulture flew away. He came back with two bright blue berries.

"Pop these into your eyes. Now tell me what you see?"

Jaguar looked around. Everything was bright and *blue* and beautiful.

"Thank you, Vulture! From now on, whenever I eat an animal, I will leave some of the bones for you.

But, when I find that Little Crab, *he* is going to be SORRY!"

But Little Crab was already hiding underneath a rock.
Jaguar never did find him.
If you go to the shore today, you will have to look hard to find Little Crab.
He is still hiding under that rock.

Source: A version of this story appears in *Twenty Tellable Tales* by Margaret Read MacDonald (American Library Association, 2005), p. 24-34. The tale is retold from *Indianermärchen aus Sudamerica* by Theodor Koch-Grünberg (Eugen Diederichs, 1927), p. 131-133, and from a telling by Augusta Baker heard in Reno, Nevada, in 1970. *Motif J2423 The eye-juggler*. See *Twenty Tellable Tales* for discussion of other variants. For another version, see "Crab with the Flying Eyes" in *Brazilian Folktales* by Livia de Almeida and Ana Portella (Libraries Unlimited, 2006), p. 41-44. This motif is often told of the Native American trickster, Coyote. For one Coyote version, see *Trickster Tales: Forty Folk Stories from Around the World* by Josepha Sherman (August House, 2005).

About Telling the Story

It is fun to extend the tale by asking the listeners what they think Little Crab's eyes saw when they sailed out.

Extending the Tale

- If you live by the coast, go to a beach and look under rocks for crabs!

- Read some other stories of characters whose eyes go flying. Talk about why someone would tell a story like this. The folklorist Barre Tolken asked his Native American friend, Yellowman, what a story about a coyote juggling his eyes meant. Barre thought it was told to explain why the coyote has yellow, runny eyes. Yellowman scoffed at that notion. He said the story was really about not fooling around with your bodily parts!

- Try some of the creative extensions mentioned above in this chapter. Add music, dance, explore through art.

Mona Monissima!
A Cuban Folktale

Mona was a little lady monkey. She was such an exuberant monkey that everyone called her "Mona Monissima!"

Mona loved to dance.
She went to the Monkey Dance every day and danced like this: *(dance wildly with lots of monkey movements)*
  "Mona! Mona MoniSSima!
  "Mona! Mona MoniSSima!
  "Mona! Mona MoniSSima!
   Uno, dos, tres y quatro!
But after a while, she got tired of dancing with the monkey boys.
She thought the human guys were *muy guapo*!
  "Why can't I dance with the HUMAN boys?"

She looked at the human girls.
  "What do they have that *I* don't have? I could look like that."
So she put on lipstick.
She put on rouge.
She put on eyebrow pencil.
She put on mascara.

  "Now look at me!"
She combed her hair.
She combed her arms.
  "Oh no…I don't think human ladies have hair on their arms."

She put on a dress with long sleeves.
  "Now look at me!"
  "Oh no…my monkey tail."

So she tied her tail in a knot around her waist.
She put on a big sash around her waist to hide the tail.
  "Now look at me! I look just like a human lady!"

She put on her high-heel shoes. THAT was difficult.

She practiced and practiced. Finally she could balance on them.

"I'm READY!"

Off she went to the dance.

The band was playing the Conga!

"Conga, Conga, Con-ga!
 Conga, Conga, Con-ga!
 Conga, Conga, Con-ga!
 Uno, dos, tres y quatro!"

Sure enough a human guy asked her to dance.

"It worked! They think I am a human lady!"

They danced and danced.

"Conga, Conga, Con-ga!
 Conga, Conga, Con-ga!
 Conga, Conga, Con-ga!
 Uno, dos, tres y quatro!"

The band played faster.

"Conga, Conga, Con-ga!
 Conga, Conga, Con-ga!
 Conga, Conga, Con-ga!
 Uno... dos... tres y quatro!"

Suddenly, Mona's tail came loose and bulged out on her side!

"WHAT...is that?" asked her dance partner.

"Oh nothing. It is just my belt. My belt came loose. Keep dancing."

So they danced and danced. Faster and faster.

"Conga, Conga, Con-ga! Conga, Conga, Con-ga! Conga, Conga, Con-ga!
 Uno... dos... tres y quatro!"

Suddenly, her tail popped out in a big bulge on her behind!

"WHAT...is that?" he asked.

"Oh nothing. It is just my petticoat. It got bunched up. Keep dancing."

"Conga, Conga, Con-ga!
Conga, Conga, Con-ga!
Conga, Conga, Con-ga!
Uno, dos, tres y quatro!"

Faster and faster they danced.
Mona forgot all about acting like a human lady. She just went wild!
She started singing and doing her monkey dance!
"Mona! Mona Monissima!
Mona! Mona Monissima!
Mona! Mona Monissima!
Uno, dos, tres y quatro!"

Suddenly, her tail came loose and dropped onto the floor!
"WHAT…is THAT?" he gasped.
"Oh NOOOO! It's my monkey tail!"

Everybody stopped. Everybody looked. Everybody shouted, "It's a MONKEY!"

Mona ran home, crying all the way.
She kicked off her shoes. She pulled off her dress.
She wiped off that makeup. She went to bed and cried and cried.

But then she heard something. It was the humans—they had come to find her.
"Mona, don't cry. We LIKED your monkey dance. Can you teach us to dance like you?
"You like my dance?"
"Yes! Teach us how to do your monkey dance!"

So everybody danced and sang together.
"Mona! Mona Monissima!
Mona! Mona Monissima!
Mona! Mona Monissima!
Uno, dos, tres y quatro!"

Mona Monissima

Nathaniel Whitman

Source: From *The Winds of Manguito: Cuban Folktales in English and Spanish! Desde los vientos de Manguito: Cuentos folklóricos de Cuba, en inglés y español* by Elvia Pérez. (Westport, CT: Libraries Unlimited), 2004. This is *Motif H151.6.2 Recognition because of imperfection of disguise.*

Extending the Tale

- Learn something about Cuba.

- What music would you hear in Cuba? Listen to some Cuban music.

- Mona was dancing to a Conga rhythm. You could line up and dance in a conga line with each person holding the waist of the person ahead of them. Your step is one-two-three-kick.

- Make up your own music for Mona's song. Make up a dance for her.

Ready...Set...Tell!

Choose a favorite tale and think of all the ways you can use this story across the arts. Make up a song and dance for each of the story's characters. Act out the story! Plan an art project that will send the story home in a visual form.

Chapter 7: CONFIDENCE—
Turning Your Students into Tellers

Because there is a natural storytelling urge and ability in all human beings, even just a little nurturing of this impulse can bring about astonishing and delightful results.

— Nancy Mellon, *The Art of Storytelling*

Once your students have been exposed to storytelling, they will be excited to let their inner storyteller out. Sharing stories is a remarkable way for students to experience success in speaking to a group. Because the art form is informal in nature and because it is best seen as a sharing rather than as performance, telling stories can help young students develop confidence in their ability to speak in front of others. An important benefit of the storytelling event is that it also lets students experience the joy of caring for an audience. It is good to stress this caring aspect of the storytelling art when working with your young tellers.

Teachers felt the chief value of the storytelling project was the way it allowed certain children to bloom, fostered group cooperation, and gave children an opportunity to be generous.

— Barbara Reed, Connecticut Storytelling Center.
School Library Journal, Oct. 87, p. 39.

Matching Students with Stories

Just as we recommend that you look through several story collections and find the stories that "speak" to you, it is important to give your students ample exposure to a variety of tales and allow them to find the story that seems like a good "fit." Even the quietest of students can find success telling a short story that they have chosen.

My students not only enjoyed hearing the stories that I shaped, but also loved shaping and telling their own tales. It honed their listening skills, fostered their creativity, and boosted their confidence in speaking before a group. I was amazed at the transformation of some of my students as they participated in storytelling. Girls who were usually soft-spoken stood in front of the class telling their tales in a dramatic voice that could be easily heard by everyone in the room.

— Joan Boyd, Grade 6, Bellevue School District, Bellevue, WA.

Techniques for Teaching Storytelling to Students

There are many ways to teach storytelling to students and the subject could easily fill several books. Here we share some of the techniques that we have used successfully over the years. Try a few out and adapt them to use in your unique setting. For more advice we highly recommend *Children Tell Stories: Teaching and Using Storytelling in the Classroom* by Martha Hamilton and Mitch Weiss (Richard C. Owen, 2005). Their book outlines how to take students through an entire storytelling unit and includes a DVD highlighting the strategies they use with student tellers.

Merry-Go-Round Telling

This is an active and sure-fire way to place a story in the heads of your students:

1. Tell your story.

2. Talk through the story structure, probably telling it over again briefly, while pointing out structural parts of the story

3. Break the students into groups of three. They should stand in a circle, facing each other.

4. Each circle chooses one person to begin the story.

5. Ring a bell as a signal to start. The beginning teller starts the story and tells until…

6. Ring the bell again. At this signal the person telling stops. The person to the first teller's left continues the story. The second teller does not begin over, but just continues where the first teller left off.

7. Ring the bell frequently, listening to see that each teller has had a chance to tell a brief but rewarding part of the tale.

8. Ring the bell to pass the story along. It passes around and around the circle.

9. Discuss the different ways to tell the story. What changed? What was most fun?

Note that every teller told in a slightly different manner. So, by the end of this exercise, each person has experienced four different storytelling styles—his or her own style, that of the others in the group, and that of you, the teacher. Remind them that ALL styles are good. Each person can tell any way he or she wants.

This technique works with any story, but is especially fun with stories that have repetition, such as "Not Our Problem" (p. 29), "Little Crab with the Magic Eyes" (p. 119), and "The Squeaky Door" (p. 158).

Tandem Telling

Students usually have a lot of fun working with a partner to share a story. This is story theater. The tellers each take a part. They act out the parts while telling the story. For example, in "Grandfather Bear is Hungry" (p. 14), the teller who takes the bear's part would say, "Grandfather Bear woke up. It was spring! He was SO hungry. He said, "I am SO HUNGRY!" So, the teller tells, while acting out the part, and speaks the parts, too.

To set this up for your students:

1. Tell the story. Select a story with just two characters.

2. Talk through the story, noting the structure and the various spoken parts.

3. Divide the group into partners. Let them decide which of the two characters each partner will take.

4. Retell the story letting the "bears" (for example) repeat Grandfather Bear's lines after you, and the "chipmunks" repeat the Chipmunk's line and actions with you.

5. If you have someone who can take the role of one of the tale's characters, demonstrate a tandem telling of the story. Often one of your students who is a quick study can take the second role. You just tell the story and pause to let your partner speak for the second character.

6. Let the duos rehearse their tale.

7. If there is time, let a few duos demonstrate for the group. Each telling will be slightly different. All the students will learn from seeing the others perform and perhaps find bits they want to incorporate into their own telling.

This is a good technique for any story with two main characters. It can also be adapted for three students by assigning one student the part of narrator, while the other two students take the speaking parts.

Cross-grade pairs: If you have a buddy class from an older or younger grade, invite that class to visit. Teach a tandem tale and let them act it out together, giving the older student the longer lines. This works especially well with a story like "Grandfather Bear," which has a long bear part and a wee chipmunk role.

Parent-student pairs: This is a fun exercise for parent's night. For preschool/K classes with parents on hand, we tell the story once, then ask the parents to stand up and act out the bear roles, while we tell it again. The children, as chipmunks, rush to feed their bears, and get five black strokes on the back in reward.

In this book, we include five tales which work well for tandem telling: "Grandfather Bear is Hungry" (p. 14), "How to Break a Bad Habit" (p. 143), "Pig and Bear Big Business" (p. 88), "The Elephants and the Bees" (p. 92), and "Koala and Tree Kangaroo" (p. 38).

Other sources for tandem tales are:

"Elk and Wren" in *Look Back and See* by Margaret Read MacDonald (NY: H.W. Wilson, 1991).

"Gunnywolf" in *Twenty Tellable Tales* by Margaret Read MacDonald (Chicago: American Library Association, 2005) and *The Gunniwolf* by Wilhelmina Harper (NY: Dutton, 1967).

"Pickin' Peas" in *Shake-it-up Tales* by Margaret Read MacDonald (Atlanta: August House, 2000) and *Pickin' Peas* by Margaret Read MacDonald, illustrated by Pat Cummins (NY: Harper Collins, 1998).

"That's Good, No That's Bad" in *Three Minute Tales* by Margaret Read MacDonald (Little Rock: August House, 2004, p. 49-50, and "Oh, That's Good! No, That's Bad" in *Stories in My Pocket: Tales Kids Can Tell* by Martha Hamilton and Mitch Weiss (Golden, CO: Fulcrum, 1996), p. 37-39.

"Toad and Horse" in *The Magic Orange Tree and Other Haitian Folktales* by Diane Wolkstein (NY: Shocken, 1997).

Acting It Out

An effective way to internalize the plot of a story is through dramatization:

1. Tell the story.

2. Assign roles and retell the story while the students move through the tale and act it out. They can speak the parts of characters, or you can feed them their lines or speak for them. It is the action that is helping them remember.

3. Break the students into small groups and let them act out the story themselves.

We often use this teaching technique with "Mabela the Clever" (p. 25), "The Squeaky Door" (p. 158), and "Old Man Wombat" (p. 106).

Mime a Story

To imprint the story in their bodies, have the students try moving through the story with no language, just telling the story with broad body movements. Have them try telling "Grandfather Bear is Hungry" without saying a word. The *body* will remember the story and help trigger the story when the student tells it with language, too. One of our New Zealand friends, the Maori teller Rangimoana Taylor, always tells a story twice for his audiences. Once with words, then he lays a finger over his lips to denote silence and retells the entire story with only his body. The effect is striking.

Telling to the Wall

Telling to the wall is a good way for students to practice a story they are working on. Facing a wall while telling, the student gets practice at projecting the voice and working on the story line. This technique works for students of all ages.

With older students, this is a fun way to quickly learn a new tale. Because we ask the students to share their stories immediately after their quick storytelling-to-the wall rehearsal, there is not time for them to worry about their performance.

Here is the sequence we use for this practice:

1. Pass out texts for short (one page) tales. We try to photocopy enough tales so that each student has a choice, a few more texts than students. We hand them out at random, but let any student exchange a tale if it does not suit. Allow 5 minutes for students to read the texts.

2. Ask the students to take their text and go face a wall somewhere in the classroom. Have them spread out so each child has a personal space for working.

3. Students should begin reading their text aloud. Ask them to think about how to interpret the story orally. Give them time to go through the story twice in this way.

4. Ask the students to put down their texts and try "telling" the story without the text. They can check back if they forget a part.

5. Ask the students to add gestures and to practice projecting their voices while pretending that an audience is just beyond the wall.

6. Have one final telling rehearsal, telling the story straight through.

7. Let the students share their newly learned story in partners or small groups. Remind them to project their voices and make eye contact. They should try to really communicate their story to the listeners.

We find George Shannon's riddle tales excellent for this exercise. You'll find lots of choices in:

Stories to Solve (Greenwillow, 2000), *More Stories to Solve* (Greenwillow, 2001) and *Still More Stories to Solve* (Greenwillow, 1996). The students just tell the riddle part of the story, but not the answer. The class then tries to guess the answer. If they can't guess, the teller gives it. This is a fun, non-threatening way to begin sharing stories.

Many of the shorter tales in Margaret Read MacDonald's *Three Minute Tales* (August House, 2005) and *Five Minute Tales* (August House, 2007) work well for this type of learning.

For older students, we use a set of "wisdom" tales" drawn from Elisa Davy Pearmain's *Doorways to the Soul: 52 Wisdom Tales from Around the World* (Pilgrim Press, 1998) and from the shortest tales in *Peace Tales: World Folktales to Talk About* by Margaret Read MacDonald (August House, 2005) and *Earth Care: World Folktales to Talk About* by Margaret Read MacDonald (August House, 2007).

Passing It Down the Line

This is a technique for rehearsing stories your class has already worked on. During this exercise suggest that the tellers focus on projecting their voices and making eye contact with the group.

Select a few students who have learned the same story and ask them to stand in front of the class.

When you clap, the teller on one end begins telling the story. Clap again and that teller stops, and the teller to his or her left continues telling, and so on down the line.

Partner Telling for Story Rehearsal

Students work with a partner and each partnership finds a quiet spot in the room to work together. Partner A tells a story to Partner B. At the end of the telling, Partner B gives feedback about what was great and what could use improvement. Then, they switch. When both partners have told their stories and received feedback, they meet briefly with you to talk about their next steps to improve their telling. When another partnership is ready, you can mix the partners up and send them off to practice again, as time allows.

Changing Partners

This is a useful technique which helps the students shape a story they have created or are trying to learn. Have the students sit in two facing rows of chairs. After each telling, the listener should ask questions of the teller, as in Partner Telling. What do they want to know more about? Did anything confuse them? What did they like most about the story?

After each student has told their story and received feedback, have the students in Row A stand and move down one chair. The new partners now exchange their stories. This can be repeated as many as three times, giving each student useful experience in orally shaping the tale, as well as useful listener feedback. Give students time to make notes about how they want to shape their story based on this experience.

Kelly Kennedy broke her third-/fourth-grade Seattle class into groups and had each group work on learning a story:

It was a great community builder, as students worked together in groups and had to work out their differences. They also had a chance to work on giving positive and constructive feedback on group performances. This gave them a sense of understanding and respecting others.

— Kelly Kennedy, Grade 3/4, Adams Elementary, Seattle, WA.

Recording the Tale

Use whatever recording technology you have available and have your students record themselves telling their stories. It's extremely helpful for students to listen to themselves telling—

and even more beneficial to see themselves telling. There are myriad ways that teachers are harnessing the power of technology to help their students assess themselves as storytellers. We know many teachers who have students record themselves independently or with a partner. Watching a video of a student teller together as a class is an invaluable way to talk about what makes strong storytelling and to help each of your tellers set goals for improving their performances. This is particularly useful if you are trying to polish stories for a big performance!

Fun Storytelling Activities

We've listed the following activities to help your students explore character and also experiment with story.

Character Press Conference

Let selected students take roles of their tale's characters. Hold a mock news conference and let other students interview the characters. This can be fun with classics such as "The Three Bears" or "Hansel and Gretel."

Mock Trial

Choose a judge, jury, and attorneys and hold a mock trial for familiar story characters, such as the wolf in "Three Little Pigs" or the wolf in "Little Red Riding Hood."

Pass the Ball

One partner tells the first sentence of a story and then passes the ball to another person. This can be played with partners, so that the story moves back and forth between them line by line. Or the story can move around a circle of students.

Go! Stop! Melt!

This is a game for working on character movement. When you say "GO!" students walk silently around the room. When you say "STOP!" everyone freezes. When you say "MELT!" students slowly melt to the ground like an ice cube. Once students understand these basics, you can insert characters in your commands, like, "GO like a RABBIT!" or "Melt like a MONKEY!" Try using different adverbs as well: "Go happily!" "Melt furiously!" This builds vocabulary and helps students try on different emotions and movements to use in their own telling.

Storytelling Cards

Prepare a deck of storytelling cards by putting interesting images on the front of cards (or cardboard squares). Have enough for each student to draw three cards, plus a few extras. The student draws three cards and makes up a story incorporating the three items depicted. You can do this rapidly in improvisational style, or deal out three cards to each student and give them time to create a story and outline it, then share it with a partner. You can adapt this game to provide separate decks with cards for setting, character, and object. The student draws one of each and creates a story around those cards.

Interrupting Partners

One partner begins improvising a story. When you ring a bell or blow a whistle, the second partner interrupts with a word. The teller must now incorporate that word into the story. For example, the teller says "A girl was going to the park…" The bell rings. The interrupting partner says, "Lobster." The teller could continue by saying, "and the girl discovered a lobster crawling across the grass…" The bell rings. The interrupting partner might then say, "Balloons." So, the teller could say, "The girl thought, 'Wouldn't it be great to give the lobster a ride on a balloon." Allow only two or three minutes for this activity, as it should be fast-paced and insane. It works best if the interrupter selects the words to use ahead of time.

Dictogloss Activity—Recreating a Story

Students listen to a story once. Then, while they listen to the story a second time, the students jot down notes quickly to remember the important details. Next, students meet with a partner and try to retell the entire story together using only each other and their notes. Finally, students listen to the story one more time and see how much of the story they were able to remember!

Circle Telling

Storytelling instructor Margaret Lippert has her students stand in two concentric circles. An outer-circle teller partners with a student in the inner-circle, and at a signal, the outer-circle teller begins to share a tale. At another signal, the teller in the outer-circle stops, and the inner-circle teller shares a tale. Then the circle shifts one place to the right and the telling repeats. This is a good technique for polishing short personal stories, or an episode of personal stories.

Drawing, Paper-folding, Handkerchief-folding, and Object Stories

Students may find it easier to begin telling stories that incorporate the manipulation of objects. This takes some of the focus off the teller. However, some dexterity is involved! We include one drawing tale at the end of this chapter, "Tommy and Sally." It makes a great tale around Halloween, as it doesn't have ghosts or other controversial elements, but *does* have a big black cat!

Here are two collections with simple manipulation stories your students might enjoy:

Pellowski, Anne. *Drawing Stories from Around the World and a Sampling of European-Handkerchief Stories*. (Westport, CT: Libraries Unlimited, 2005). Pellowski, Anne. *The Story Vine: A Sourcebook of Unusual and Easy-to-Tell Stories from Around the World*. (New York: Aladdin, 2008).

Sharing Personal Stories

Here is a technique for creating a personal story to share. You can use this process to prepare your own story to demonstrate for your students and then use the technique to teach your students how to shape their own personal story.

1. Brainstorm a list of topics from your life about which you could tell a story: funny things that happened to you, mishaps, family events that went awry, travel tales. Think in particular about stories from your own childhood.

2. Look over the list and choose one story you would like to tell to your students.

3. Think over this story and decide how you should open it. Consider the ending, as it is hard to get a story to end on just the right note.

4. Go over the whole story in your mind. Speak it out loud if you want.

5. Now tell the story to a friend. Ask the friend what they would like to know more about. Were any parts of the story confusing to them? What was their favorite part of the story?

6. Think about ways you want to change your telling to make the story more effective.

7. Try the story out on another friend.

8. Now tell it to your class. If you are introducing a unit on personal storytelling, this is a good time to let *them* critique *your* story.

To help your students create their own personal stories, follow the same steps you just used. Write the story down if you like.

On the final days of rehearsal, the students can tell their story out loud to the wall for practice. Then, they will be ready to tell the story to the whole class.

Feedback for Improvement

We all strive to give timely feedback to our students and it's important that we provide our budding storytellers with input that will help them develop their skills. Many teachers use some form of storytelling rubric as a tool for students to evaluate themselves and each other. If you're involved in a storytelling unit, the same rubric could be the basis for an end of unit assessment. We find it useful to create these rubrics with our students, based on the elements of storytelling that we're focusing on at the time. We've listed a few aspects of storytelling that you could incorporate into your own storytelling rubrics:

Voice

- Expression—Does the teller use an expressive voice?

- Fluency—Is the telling smooth and fluent?

- Pacing—Does the teller speed up and slow down the pace at appropriate times?

- Volume—Is the teller heard by everyone in the room?

- Clarity—Is the teller using a voice that is understandable to everyone?

- Characterization—Does the teller convey emotions effectively through vocalization, or mood of telling for different characters?

Body

- Posture—Does the teller stand confidently while telling?

- Gestures—Does the teller use focused gestures or movements that support the story?

- Facial Expressions—Does the teller use an expressive face to help convey meaning?

- Eye Contact—Does the teller make eye contact with everyone in the audience?

Story

- Beginning—Does the teller start with a clear, confident opening line?

- Word Choice—Does the teller incorporate interesting vocabulary in the telling?

- Imagery—Does the teller paint a picture for the listener?

- Sequencing—Does the teller shape the tale with a clear beginning, middle, and end?

- Ending—Does the teller end the story confidently, with a sense of closure?

Showcasing the Stories

Once you feel confident that your students are growing as storytellers, it's time to have them share their stories beyond the classroom! Here are a few ideas for helping your students bring their stories to the greater community.

Share Your Tales with Another Class

Once your students have refined their telling of some tales, take them to another class to let them share their stories. Letting your students share with younger classes brings them a lot of status. The Kindergarteners will make your older students feel like stars and taking your Kindergarteners to tell to the older kids will do the same for them!

If your class has a buddy classroom, storytelling is a great way to share with them. One fifth-grade class learned to tell "Little Crab with the Magic Eyes." The students decorated their classroom with an undersea motif and then they invited their Kindergarten buddies in for a story experience. Each fifth grader took their Kindergarten buddy, sat them down on a specially drawn paper "coral rock" and told them the story, while seaweed dangled above.

Good Morning Storytelling

If your students are just starting out, a nice way to allow them to share their telling with their families is to invite just a few families in each morning to hear their children tell as a part of your morning meeting routine. Often, both parents are busy with work, but we find that if we give families enough advanced notice, many moms and dads are able to arrange their morning so that they can spend a few extra minutes at school before they head off to work. You can have a Good Morning Storytelling series and have just the parents of three or four students come into class on a given morning to hear their children tell their story. This allows for a more informal storytelling experience.

Family Storytelling Evening

When your students are feeling more confident as tellers, you might plan to have a big storytelling evening or an afternoon tea. Students can tell for all of the parents and children. This works well as the culmination of a storytelling unit or as a year-end celebration, if you have been telling stories all year. You have to be sure that each of the stories is quite short and to program your event so that your strongest tellers begin and end the storytelling concert. Have parents bring treats and plan for an intermission, as everyone needs a break from listening after a while. If you plan a large event like this, it's a good idea to set up a sound system, which gives your students practice working with a microphone. Be sure to rehearse with the microphones at least once before the big performance.

Parent-Child Storytelling Class

Try offering a parent-child storytelling class some evening. Let parents and their children work together to learn tandem folktales and act them out. You could share one of your favorite bedtime tales, help them learn to tell it in-the-round, and give them a copy of the text to take home. Send them home with more stories to play with together as a family.

Storytelling Festival

Once you have been telling in your school for a while, you may find storytelling is contagious. If you get a big storytelling buzz started in your school, why not consider starting your own storytelling festival? This could be done on a small scale—with just a few students telling one evening—or dream big! We know of several schools that invite local professional tellers to work with their students and then showcase both the students and the performers at a large event. The whole school community could be invited to listen to small groups of tellers in different areas of the school with a schedule provided. This could be linked with another school activity, like a school carnival, to boost attendance. Or create a storytelling benefit performance for your PTA.

Training Your Tellers: Sources to Get Started

Here are resources giving good advice from tellers who have experience teaching children and teens to tell.

Collins, Rives and Pamela J. Cooper, *The Power of Story: Teaching through Storytelling*. Long-Grove, III: Waveland Press, Inc., 1997. 2nd edition. Originally titled *Look What Hap-*

pened to Frog. Information on selecting, learning, telling, and dramatizing tales is provided, along with many activities for classroom storytelling groups. Interviews with several tellers are included.

Hamilton, Martha and Mitch Weiss. *Children Tell Stories. Teaching and Using Storytelling in the Classroom.* 2nd ed. Katonah, New York: Richard C. Owen, 2005. Everything you need to know to teach your students to tell stories is provided, including a DVD of student tellers. See also the authors' simple texts for student tellers: *Stories in My Pocket: Tales Kids Can Tell.* Golden, CO: Fulcrum, 1996 and *How & Why Stories: World Tales Kids Can Read & Tell.* Little Rock: August House, 1999.

Haven, Kendall. *Super Simple Storytelling: A Can-Do Guide for Every Classroom, Every Day.* Greenwood, CO: Libraries Unlimited, 2000. This covers learning and performing tales, as well as using storytelling in the curriculum. Half of this book features activities for student storytelling groups.

Rubinstein, Robert. *Curtains Up! Theatre Games and Storytelling.* Golden, CO: Fulcrum, 2000. The focus is on theatre games to warm up student storytellers but there is also one chapter on training student storytellers.

Let's Look at Grandfather Bear

Teach your students to tell Grandfather Bear in tandem, using the techniques outlined above. Have fun with a whole noisy roomful of hungry bears and helpful chipmunks! Search the school for audiences, so your new stars can share their stories.

Try a Tale!

Here are two very easy stories for your students to begin with. Let them tell "How to Break a Bad Habit" in teams. After telling with a partner, each student should be able to easily tell the whole story solo. For the simplest telling begin them with "Tommy and Sally." After hearing this story a couple of times and copying your drawing, students can take it home and share it with confidence.

How to Break a Bad Habit
A West African Folktale

Monkey and Rabbit sat talking.
Monkey was scratching.
Rabbit was twitching.

"Would you STOP that TWITCHING," said Monkey. "What a bad HABIT."

"Bad HABIT?" said Rabbit. "Talk about BAD HABITS. Look at YOU.
Scratch…scratch…scratch…Now, THAT is a bad habit."

"Well I could easily STOP if I wanted to," said Monkey.
"So could I" said Rabbit.

"We'll SEE!" said Monkey. "Let's have a contest.
The first person to scratch or twitch LOSES.
Begin…when…I…say…GO!

"One, two, three—GO!"

Rabbit sat very still. Monkey sat very still.
Monkey did not scratch. Rabbit did not twitch.
Monkey really wanted to scratch.
Rabbit really wanted to twitch.

Monkey really REALLY wanted to scratch.
Rabbit really REALLY wanted to twitch.

"I have an idea!" Monkey was excited.
"Let's tell stories." And Monkey began to talk.

"Yesterday I was walking down the road.
A little boy threw rocks at me.
Guess where he hit me?
He hit me *here*." Monkey scratched his nose.

"He hit me *here*." Monkey scratched his leg.

"And here, and here, and here." Monkey was scratching all over.

"Wait! Wait! *I* know a story!" said Rabbit.

"Yesterday I was walking in the swamp.

And mosquitoes bit me. One bit me *here*." Rabbit twitched his nose.

"One bit me *here*." Rabbit twitched his ear.

"Another bit me *here*." Rabbit twitched his other ear.

"And here, and here, and here." Rabbit was twitching all over.

Rabbit and Monkey began to laugh. They laughed and laughed.

"Let's keep our bad habits and just be friends," they said.

Source: *Twenty Tellable Tales: Audience Participation Folktales for the Beginning Storyteller* by Margaret Read MacDonald (Chicago: American Library Association, 2004). A West African folktale. *Motif K263 Agreement not to scratch. In talking the trickster makes gestures and scratches without detection.*

About Telling This Story: Use lots of actions when you tell this. Twitch your nose, when you are Rabbit. Put your hands up as ears and twitch them. And, of course, scratch a lot when you are Monkey. This story is fun to tell with a partner; each takes one role.

Extending the Tale

- Tell the children that on the count of three they must sit up straight. Nobody can scratch. Nobody can twitch. "1, 2, 3, START!" After a while, ask if their back is starting to itch…their leg? Tell them that if anyone wants to move, they must tell a story like Monkey and Rabbit did that will allow them to make a gesture. Demonstrate with your own short story if you need to. Example: "Yesterday I was working in my garden and a bee stung me. He stung me here! And here!" Once they get started, the entire class will want to tell their own story. This allows them all to tell a very brief story in a non-threatening environment.

- Discuss bad habits and possible ways to break them.

- Discuss the importance of accepting your friends' foibles.

Tommy and Sally
A Drawing Story from Appalachia

Once there was a boy named Tommy.

Here is a "T." "T" stands for Tommy.

Tommy had a friend named Sally.
What letter do we need for Sally? "S"—

"S" is for Sally.

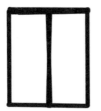

Tommy decided to build himself a house.

He built a wall here…and a wall here…a floor here…

What else does he need for his house?

A window—yes.

A door—yes.

A roof.

Oh, and it was very cold there, so he needed chimneys for the fireplaces.
One for this room and one for that room.

Tommy planted some grass around his door, so it would look pretty.

He said, "I am going to go tell Sally about my new house!"

So he walked over to Sally's house.

He said, "Come over and see my new house!"

"OK!" said Sally. "But let's go down in the basement and get some apples out of the apple basket to eat on the way."

So they went down in the basement and got some apples.

They came out the basement door and took two steps—and they fell down in a mud-puddle!

They went along over to Tommy's house and—fell down in a mud-puddle!

Took two steps and—what do you think happened to those kids?

They fell down in a mud-puddle again!

They got almost up to Tommy's house and Sally said, "I'm not going to go in that house!"

"Why not?" said Tommy.

"I'm afraid of that BIG BLACK CAT!"

Source: "The Tale of a Black Cat" in *When the Lights Go Out: 20 Scary Tales to Tell* by Margaret Read MacDonald. (New York: H.W. Wilson, 1988) p. 155-158. That book cites eight other variants of this tale.

Extending the Tale

- Retell the tale, pausing to allow your students to draw their own cat along with you.

- Pair your students with partners and have them take turns telling the story to each other.

- Provide black construction paper and white chalk for the students to draw their own cat tale. Or use black marker on orange paper for a nod to Halloween, when appropriate. These make a nice October bulletin board.

- Once your students are telling "Tommy and Sally" confidently, can they use other letters to make up their own story?

Ready...Set...Tell!

Think about your own classroom setting. How can you give your students opportunities to be storytellers? Try a couple of the activities suggested in this chapter and see where your students take their own stories. Think of what areas of storytelling performance you'd like to focus on and create a storytelling rubric with your class to guide your work with storytelling together. When your students are ready find a way to help them showcase their tales!

Chapter 8: Storytelling and Learning a New Language

Storytelling is among the oldest forms of communication. Storytelling is the commonality of all human beings, in all places, in all times.

— Rives Collins, *The Power of Story: Teaching Through Storytelling*

This summer I taught English language learners. I was given a curriculum that was much too difficult. It was not going to teach the students language/vocabulary as much as it was going to help them stumble. I began telling stories to get them to use language. Retelling the story and acting it out. I had seven different languages and 18 students in summer school. Pantomiming was hysterical to teach a vocabulary word. But since it came from the story, the students were able to grasp the meaning and use it in context.

— Tena Kilroy, Elizabeth Blackwell Elementary, Redmond, WA.

Storytelling offers a wonderful way for students who are new to a language to develop their vocabulary and comprehension. It's a remarkable tool that helps scaffold language for those students who are learning English in your classroom. In this section we will use a variety of terms interchangeably referring to English-language instruction: EAL (English as Additional Language): ELL (English Language Learners): SEI (Sheltered English Immersion). Whatever you call your English-language program, storytelling will enhance your work with students. These storytelling techniques are also equally useful for teaching Spanish, French, Chinese, Japanese, Arabic—ANY language instruction program can be enriched with storytelling.

Simple folktales are a perfect tool for giving beginning language learners practice in their new language because they help students develop both their receptive and productive language skills. When the tales are told in simple language, students not only listen and comprehend, they also find success joining in during the telling and, eventually, retelling the tales on their own. The refrains embedded in many folktales allow for joyful repetition of key phrases. What a fun way to learn a new language!

I guess I was thinking storytelling would just have entertainment value, but it is really great for all of my readers that range from first-grade/ELL level readers to fifth-grade readers. It gives them equal standing.

— Kelly Kennedy, Grade 3/4, Adams Elementary, Seattle, WA.

Give Me a Break!

If you have ever tried to immerse yourself in a new language, you know how tiring it can be to try to think in that language for an hour, let alone an entire day. What a relief it is when there is a phrase you recognize. Pattern stories can offer that moment of recognition and relief for the language learners in your classroom. Stories with very simple language are accessible to everyone. Your EAL students can relax into the story and participate in the telling successfully.

I was truly amazed with my student responses. My groups include speakers from at least ten different languages and twenty different countries. Everyone of my ELL students loved hearing and retelling these stories with me. We enjoyed putting motions to the stories and acting them out. Since many of my students enter the classroom in what we ELL teachers call the "silent period of language development," this really broke the ice for them. Now even my newest ELL students are more able to speak about events in their own lives and write them down.

— Susan Ramos, ELL 1-4, Challenger Elementary, Mukilteo, WA

Sampling Other Languages:
Once Upon a Time, *Il y Avait Une Fois, Mukashi Mukashi*

If there are students in your class who speak another language, sharing a story with some words or the entire tale in their home language is a great gift for them. Taking the time to tell a story in a student's mother tongue sends a powerful message that you value her language and her culture. It's a perfect way for other students in the class to gain insights into their classmate's culture. You can learn a simple story yourself in their language, or invite a bilingual person into the classroom who can tandem tell with you and translate as you tell.

A very simple story, such as "Two Goats on a Bridge," at the end of this chapter, can be taught to the whole class easily by having them repeat each line after you. The story is perfect for tandem telling with a partner who speaks another language. You say a word in English. The second teller says the word in the second language. All your students repeat in the second language. For a video of Margaret and Thai storyteller Wajuppa Tossa telling this story in two languages see the link in the "Extensions" after the "Two Goats on a Bridge" text below. The key is to learn the story well yourself. Choose a person who is bilingual for a partner. Often one of your students can do this with you. Practice a bit first, then perform for the class. You say a line in English. Your partner says the same line in Spanish or Chinese or….Once the pattern is understood, the students can take the tale home and have their families help them retell it in their own languages, then come back and share it with the class in Japanese, in Arabic or….What a delight for everyone!

———————————

I have given a copy of "Two Goats on a Bridge" to my ELL students and their parents are teaching them the words in the story that they don't already know. They have been telling this story in class when they are ready. Mind you these are first-and second-grade students working with me to tell this story, and it has been a blast. So far, one Spanish speaker and one Vietnamese speaker have been able to share the story in their home language.

— Kasey Clay, Covington Elementary, Covington, Washington

———————————

Bilingual Classrooms

In bilingual classrooms there is a wonderful opportunity for teachers to work together to tell stories in two languages. If you are competent in a second language, you could tell stories bilingually yourself. If not, you could always team with a teaching partner who is fluent in another language and you can tell the story together. Telling in two languages at once can be fluid and delightful. To do this effectively, the teller needs to pause after each phrase to let the other language flow in. It is a balancing act as you both listen closely to each other and share in the telling.

Jen and Nat worked with two Mandarin-speaking teachers at Hong Kong International School to tell "Mabela the Clever" for a school assembly. Though the students were all studying Mandarin, most had a limited vocabulary. By teaching them the chant in Mandarin before the story started, the student body was able to chant along with Mabela, ending in a resounding "Hòu miàn!" To read more about this event and to see the Mandarin text they used, see "Mabela the Clever in Hong Kong" in *Tell the World: Storytelling Across Language Barriers* by Margaret Read MacDonald (Libraries Unlimited, 2008) p. 67-71. This book will also give you several hints on how to tell through a translator.

Kinesthetic Connection

We worked with a talented colleague, Megan Chadwick, who is an EAL teacher, yoga instructor, and avid storyteller. She blends these talents to great effect by guiding her EAL students to create simple stories with strong, clear movements. The students quickly learn to retell their story when they match the vocabulary to physical movement. When your body moves in sync with a story, your body learns the tale, too! The repeated motion helps your mind pull up the vocabulary and intonation for the story.

Sharing Stories from Their Own Cultures

Many EAL teachers have had success asking students to retell or write down folktales from their home countries. Often families can share such stories with the students, and this gives the student a special offering to bring to class. For students who have trouble discovering stories from their home culture, you can ask your librarian to help locate stories from that culture. You can also find stories online, but these online versions are often not told very elegantly, nor in simple English either, so they may need some rewording to make them tellable for your students. One UK source gives brief bilingual folktales from 21 cultures: www.worldstories.org.uk.

Storytelling in Sign Language

Because the stories we suggest are so simple, repetitive, and fun to tell, parents and teachers using sign language find them a delightful way to incorporate storytelling with their children. The simplicity of the language in these tales and their patterning make tale sharing easily accessible to even a basic-skills-level signing teller.

Shaping a Story for Telling with Second Language Learners

JonLee Joseph, who teaches at the Salalah College of Technology in Oman, suggests these steps for simplifying a folktale for use with second language learners. Any short, repetitive folktale can easily be adapted following these steps.

1. Select simple stories with a straightforward plot line.

2. Tales with repetition are especially useful as the same language is repeated over and over. Be sure to repeat the language exactly the same way each time.

3. Simplify the language. Avoid colloquialisms.

4. Use short sentences.

5. Keep your telling focused on the plot. Details of imagery and characterization are not as important as comprehension at this point.

6. Make a list of key vocabulary to teach before telling the tale.

Teaching a Second Language Through Story

Here is a possible structure for learning a story in a second language. We are using Spanish instruction as a model here, but this simple story can be used to teach any language.

For students with almost no language skills, begin by telling the story mostly in the student's first language. Insert a few of the key words in the second language. Retell the story again the next day and insert more of the second language vocabulary. After a few retellings, you can now share the entire story in the second language. The same techniques work for teaching EAL or when teaching a second language to English speakers. For example, you want to teach your students to tell "The Squeaky Door" (p. 158) in Spanish.

First Day: Tell the story in English, but insert the Spanish words for "No! Not me!" ("¡NO! ¡YO NO!"). Students repeat after you both the English phrases and the new Spanish words. Be sure the students repeat after you the English phrases, "Kissed the boy goodnight. Tiptoed out. Turned off the light."

Second Day: Tell the story again in English, but now replace with Spanish the English phrases, "Kissed the boy goodnight. Tiptoed out. Turned off the light." The students repeat each phrase in Spanish AFTER you say it. "Besó al niño. Salió de puntillas. Apagó la luz." Your actions show what is happening. And they will already know the story from the previous day's telling.

Third Day: Tell the story entirely in Spanish. Call students up to act out the parts of the boy and animals. Have them create a pocket story with simple drawings and write in key words in Spanish.

Fourth Day: Using their pocket stories and working in teams, let the students try to "tell" the story to each other in Spanish.

The key is for the teacher to tell the tale in very simple language using lots of gestures to convey the tale's meaning. Choose very simple stories with repetitive language and refrains in which the students can join. Repeat the tale several times as demonstration. Try to tell the tale with the same words each time.

You may have to rewrite your stories slightly to keep the vocabulary as simple as possible. Most of the stories included in this book have been rewritten in fairly basic language and can be used for EAL with just a bit more tweaking. You will be able to shape other stories for EAL use, with a bit of work.

Spanish language texts for "The Squeaky Door," "Two Goats on a Bridge," "Not Our Problem," "Ms. Cricket Gets Married," "How to Break a Bad Habit," "Frog and Locust Call For Rain," and "Grandfather Bear is Hungry" are available at www.margaretreadmacdonald.com. Click on BOOKS, then click on *Teaching with Story*.

Let's Look at Grandfather Bear

When telling stories as a vehicle for learning English or another language, it is important to pare the language down to the basics. Making the language as simple and as direct as possible will make the story easier to remember. The wording of "Grandfather Bear" in this book has already been simplified for easy learning and would work fairly well for EAL students in that format. But look at the story from which we took that text:

"In the spring, when the warm sun began to shine on bear's cave, Bear woke up and came out into the sunshine. Ooohhh…he felt…HUNGRY! Bear had not eaten a thing all winter long. "I am so HUNGRY!" growled Bear. Bear lumbered down to the berry patch."

To make the story easier to learn, we cut out the introductory sentence entirely and changed words like "growled" and "lumbered."

Try a Tale!

One of our favorite stories to use with beginning English speakers is "The Squeaky Door." The repetition of simple phrases allows students with extremely limited language to join in almost immediately and everyone can make the animal noises together right away. This is a story that works well with younger students and with older students who are just delighted to have a tale they can follow.

Working in Thailand, Margaret found this tale especially useful for sixth-grade beginning English learners. Because the final consonants in many Thai words are not sounded, this story's repeated phrases were very useful for emphasizing those final sounded consonants in many words. "TiptoeD out," "TurneD off the light," CloseD the door," KisseD the boy good-night." And while working in Jamaica, Margaret discovered that students had trouble writing in the past tense. So she used this story and encouraged all to repeat the "ed" words each time in an attempt to stress the use of the past tense form.

Our second example below, "Two Goats on a Bridge," makes a wonderful story for easy language learning. And it is a good choice for students to share in their own languages. We have had amazing reports from teachers who used this tale to validate their students' many home languages. It has been shared by children in Hindi, Tagalog, Arabic, Ukranian, Salish and Mandarin—to mention just a few!

The Squeaky Door
A Folktale from Puerto Rico

Little Boy went to Grandma's house to spend the night.
Grandma said, "You get to sleep in the big bed tonight all by yourself.
Will you be scared?"
Little Boy said, "NO, not ME!"
So Grandma tucked the boy in.
She kissed the boy goodnight.
"Now, when I go out and close the door and turn off the light…will you be scared?"
"NO! Not ME!"

So Grandma tiptoed out.
She turned off the light. "Click."
She closed the door. "SQUEEEAK!"

Boy began to cry! "WAAAHHHH!"
"Oh no! Were you scared?"
Little Boy whispered, "No…not me."
"Hmmm. I think you were scared.
Do you want to sleep with the cat?"
"YES! YES! YES!"

So Grandma brought the cat in.
Grandma kissed the cat goodnight, "SMACK!"
She kissed the boy goodnight, "SMACK!"
"Now when I go out and close the door and turn off the light…will you be scared?"
"NO. Not ME!"
Grandma tiptoed out.
She turned off the light. "Click"
She closed the door. "SQUEEEEAK!"
Boy began to cry! "WAAAAHHHH!"
Cat began to meow! "MEOWWW!"
"Oh no! Were you scared?"
"No. Not me."
"Would you like to sleep with the dog?"
"YES! YES! YES!"

So grandma brought the dog in.
Grandma kissed the boy goodnight. "SMACK!"
She kissed the cat goodnight. "SMACK!"
She kissed the dog goodnight. "SMACK!"
"When I go out and close the door and turn off the light...will you be scared?"
"NO, not ME!"

Grandma tiptoed out.
She turned off the light. "Click"
She closed the door. "SQUEEEAK!"
"WAAAAHHH!"
"MEOW!"
"WOOF! WOOF! WOOF!"
"Oh no! Were you scared?"
"No. Not me."
Would you like to sleep with the pig?"
"YES! YES! YES!"

Grandma brought the pig in.
Grandma kissed the boy goodnight. "SMACK!"
She kissed the cat goodnight. "SMACK!"
She kissed the dog goodnight. "SMACK!"
She kissed the pig goodnight. "SMACK!"
"When I go out and close the door and turn off the lights...will you be scared?"
"NO! Not ME!"

Grandma tiptoed out.
She turned off the light. "Click."
She closed the door. "SQUEEEAK!"
"WAAAAHHH!"
"MEOW!"
"WOOF! WOOF! WOOF!"
"OINK! OINK OINK!"
"Oh, no! Were you scared?"
"No. Not me."
"Would you like to sleep with the HORSE?"
"YES! YES! YES!"

So Grandma brought the horse in.
Grandma kissed the boy goodnight. "SMACK!"
She kissed the cat goodnight. "SMACK!"
She kissed the dog goodnight. "SMACK!"
She kissed the pig goodnight. "SMACK!"
She kissed the horse goodnight. "SMACK!"
"When I go out and close the door and turn off the lights…will you be scared?"
"NO! Not ME!"
So Grandma tiptoed out.
She turned off the light. "Click."
She closed the door. "SQUEEEAK!"
"WAAAAHHH!"
"MEOW!"
"WOOF! WOOF! WOOF!"
"OINK! OINK OINK!"
"NEIGH! NEIGH! NEIGH!"
The animals began to jump up and down in the bed!
"KABOOM!" The bed broke.

"Oh, my goodness.
This will never do.
This will never do."
Grandma put the horse back.
She put the pig back.
She put the dog back.
She put the cat back.

She took Little Boy to sleep with her and Grandpa that night.

And next morning,
Grandma got out her tool chest.
And she FIXED that broken bed.
Then she got out her oil can.
And she OILED that squeaky door.
"SQUEE…SQUEE…" "glub…glub…glub…glub…"
"Squee…squee…" "glub…glub…glub…glub…"
"Squee…squee…" "glub…glub…glub…glub…" *[speak more softly each time you 'Squee…']*

[Silence as door is quietly moved back and forth, then a smile.]

And that night, when Grandma put Little Boy to bed…
She kissed the boy goodnight. "SMACK!"
She kissed the cat goodnight. "SMACK!"
Nobody else!
"When I go out and close the door and turn off the light…will you be scared?"
"NO! Not ME!"
Grandma tiptoed out.
She turned off the light. "Click"
She closed the door. *[No sound]*
She listened.
She heard LIttle Boy—snoring. Ahnhmmmm…Ahnhmmmm…

She listened.
She heard the cat—snoring. Ahnhmmmm…Ahnhmmmm…
And that's the story of Grandma, Little Boy, and the SQUEAKY door!

Source: *Parent's Guide to Storytelling* by Margaret Read MacDonald (Atlanta: August House, 2001) and the picture book *The Squeaky Door* by Margaret Read MacDonald. Illus. by Mary Newell DePalma (New York: Harper Collins, 2006). The story is based on a Puerto Rican folksong, "La Cama." A version appears in *Folklore portorriqueño* by Rafael Ramirez de Arellano (Madrid: Centro de Estudios Históricas, 1926). *Motif Z49.17 Little boy under bed given animals to comfort.*

Extending the Tale

- Draw a bed, showing it from the foot of the bed with pillows and blanket. Paste this picture on another piece of paper, then cut a slit along the top of the blanket. Make cutouts of the boy, dog, cat, pig, and horse. The children can retell the story as they tuck the animals under the blanket. If you have access to the picture book, *The Squeaky Door*, just copy the illustrations of the bed and animals.

- And of course, act this story out! Bring up as many children ("animals") as you like to stuff in the bed. Margaret once had 39 animals in the bed at a Singapore library telling. You can provide a blanket and let the kids have fun acting this out on their own later.

- Talk about the noises the animals make in the story. What noises do these same animals make in the children's home languages?

Two Goats on a Bridge
Story Number One

[Ask the audience to repeat everything you say and do everything you do.]
Hill. *[Hold up right fist.]*
Hill. *[Hold up left fist.]*
Goat. *[Hold up right index finger.]*
Goat. *[Hold up left index finger.]*
One day.
Goat went down. *[Right finger goes down to waist level.]*
Crossed the bridge. *[Right finger crosses at waist level.]*
Ate the grass. Mnnnnnn. *[Finger wiggles and you make munching sounds.]*
Went back. *[Right finger retraces steps back to shoulder level.]*

One day. *[Left finger repeats actions, as above.]*
Goat went down.
Crossed the bridge.
Ate the grass.
Went back.

One day.
Both goats went down. *[Both fingers repeat above actions.]*
Both goats crossed the bridge. *[Both fingers meet on the bridge.]*
"Hey! I want to cross!"
"I want to cross!"
"I'm bigger!"
"I'm stronger!" *[Fingers push against each other.]*
"ANNNNNHHHHH"
And they FELL into the river. *[Drop hands to sides.]*

[Goats climb out muttering.]
"He did not cooperate!" *[Two fingers face away from each other and leave.]*
"He did not cooperate!"

Story number two [teller announces second story]

[Repeat all actions as in Story Number One.]
Hill.
Hill.
Goat.
Goat.

One day.
Goat came down.
Crossed the bridge.
Ate the grass.
Went back.

One day.
Goat came down.
Crossed the bridge.
Ate the grass.
Went back.

One day.
Both goats came down.
Both goats crossed the bridge.

"Hey! I want to cross."
"I want to cross!"
"Oh, oh."
"We have a problem!"
"What can we do?"
"Let's see…"

Maybe if we both squeezed…
We could both pass? *[Squeeze two fingers past each other.]*

"Nnnnnnhhhhh…YES!"
"He cooperated!" [Fingers nod at each other.]
"He cooperated!"

Now the question is:
What kind of goat are you?

Source: *Three Minute Tales* by Margaret Read MacDonald (Atlanta: August House, 2004). A longer version can be found in *Peace Tales: World Folktales to Talk About* (Atlanta: August House, 1992). This story is a combination of two folktales, which have been abbreviated and combined with hand motions. The un-cooperative goat story is found in Mirra Ginsburg, *Three Rolls and One Doughnut: Fables from Russia* (New York: Dial, 1970). The cooperative goat tale was recorded by the 16th century German Scholar, Johannes Pauli, in *Shimpf und Ernst* (Thann, 1592). *Motif J133.1. One wild goat steps over another. They thus pass each other uninjured on a cliff. This shows advantage of peacefulness.*

Extending the Tale

- See Margaret Read MacDonald and Wajuppa Tossa tell this story in English and Lao at www.youtube.com/watch?v=KzbK9Bu8LIA (Story Number One)

- www.youtube.com/watch?v=nrKG-fw50k&feature=related&pos=0 (Story Number Two)

- Learn the story in Spanish: See www.margaretreadmacdonald.com. Click on BOOKS. Click on *Teaching with Story*.

- With the help of your students, make a language chart and compare words and phrases of this story from several languages. "Hill. Colina. Bukit. Shan. Pu."

Ready…Set…Tell!

Take any short tale you love and try paring down the language to the basics. How simple can you make the phrases? Try telling it with your students this week. Do you work with a teacher at school who could tell with you in a different language? Take a tale from this book and try telling it bilingually together. Your students will be delighted!

Chapter 9: Storytelling for Special Needs Audiences

"After nourishment, shelter and companionship, stories are the thing we need most in the world."

— Philip Pullman

All children love story and we have found that students with a wide range of learning needs respond enthusiastically to storytelling. There is something about the structure of a story that allows it to enter the mind more easily than ordinary talk. Simply by looking directly into the child's eyes and animatedly telling a story, sometimes an unexpected engagement can take place. Whether you work with inclusion children in your mainstream classroom or you teach a pull-out class for children with extreme needs, you can use storytelling successfully with your students.

Jen and Nat tell stories every summer in the King County Library System. When they first began telling in libraries, fifteen years ago, a young boy attended one of their shows. He sat riveted during the performance. After the show, his mother explained that he was autistic and that she was pleased to see him so engaged during the performance. The following summer, the same boy was in the audience again. This time, his mom shared that he had loved the stories from last year and had told and retold them for weeks and weeks. The next year, he was right back in the audience. Fast forward fifteen years and this young boy is now a young man with a job, yet every summer he and his mother still come back to hear more stories at the library. Stories have the power to connect with all children deeply. Sometimes, that connection is fleeting, but other times it can last a lifetime. And often, we never know what impact one small story has had on the life of a child.

As storytellers, we have seen children excited about stories in a variety of inclusion and pull-out settings. As teachers, we have limited experience working with special needs students, but we have received feedback from Special Education teachers over the years who have been successful using storytelling in a variety of creative ways. We include some of their suggestions here and hope they will inspire you to adapt storytelling strategies to your own unique situation.

Use Simple Stories with Repeated Motion

This is the perfect fit for the collaboration model I was hoping to establish… so many possibilities of how to use storytelling and movement combined to enhance and teach in all areas of the curriculum.

— Tamara Osborn, Itinerant Physical Therapist, Mukilteo School District, Mulkilteo, WA.

Stories with repetitive motions can be great for helping children develop motor skills. Here are just a few suggestions for using stories in this book to incorporate broad movements.

When telling "Koala and Tree Kangaroo" (p. 38), encourage broad arm lifts as the animals go "over a mountain and down a valley." Let everyone dig with Tree Kangaroo.

When telling "The Squeaky Door," encourage everyone to chime in on "NO! Not ME!" while shaking their heads. Use broad arm movements to close the squeaky door, while calling out, "SQUEEEAK!" Raise an arm to "click" off the light.

Try telling "Monkeys in the Rain" (p. 170) and similar stories with lots of physical action, asking the children to make the movements with you. This can improve bilateral coordination and physical awareness.

Physical Therapist, Tamara Osborn told "Monkeys in the Rain" with two Kindergarten boys with gross motor delays to enhance their motor learning and participation. Tamara wrote, *"Both boys were saying the story and doing the actions right along with me! They clearly enjoyed the story and worked hard at all the different actions."*

Link Stories with Physical Activities

After telling "Two Goats on a Bridge," (p. 162), let students walk low balance beams. Place two balance beams together and have pairs of children help each other cross without falling. Tamara Osborn used this technique and also created a "cooperative-uncooperative" poster. The children put their picture up on the cooperative side if they worked together well. As a result, the activity stressed both cooperation and balancing skills.

After telling "Old Man Wombat," (p. 106), let the children all stand and move around the room as you retell the story. They can hop with Mother Kangaroo, or bend over and walk slowly with eyes almost closed as Old Man Wombat moves forward.

Act out "Mabela, the Clever" (p. 38), as suggested on page 25, or let some of the students be mice and some can be cats (their choice). As you retell the story and sing the song, the mice tiptoe and the cats sneak up.

Use Manipulatives

Spokane, Washington, teacher Anna Owens let her students select Tinker Toy pieces to use as "pretend fiddles and hoes" while she told the Aesop fable of the Grasshopper and the Ant. When the Grasshopper fiddled repeatedly, the students did the same. When Ant worked hard at his digging, the students used their Tinker Toy pieces to pretend to dig.

Role Play the Stories

After hearing the story of "The Three Bears" a few times, Anna Owens wanted to guide her students through an enactment of the tale. One girl was not likely to be able to work with the other students cooperatively. So, Anna privately asked this girl if she would like to play the role of Goldilocks. Then, while the others were out at recess, Owens guided this girl as she pretended to eat the porridge, break the chair, mess up the beds, and fall asleep in one of the beds. When the students returned from recess, they were surprised to discover that Goldilocks had been in their classroom! Now, they played the part of the bears and finally discovered Goldilocks in the bedroom asleep.

Modify the Pace of Your Telling

Most of the stories in this book are simple and repetitive. Practice telling these tales at a slow and deliberate pace. Use your most exciting voices to enhance the story. And don't give up if the event seems to fall flat. Students often are internalizing more than we realize.

Special Education teacher, Wendy Little, used the tale of "Grandmother Spider" with her class. A few days later, while she was telling a simple participation tale, "Swim Little Mouse," one-on-one to a student, a boy from her class came up and said, "Find the light and spider, Miss Wendy." She was amazed because he had trouble verbalizing his needs. And at first she didn't realize that he was asking her to tell him the story. She told it very slowly, as she could see that he was really trying to internalize it. She writes: "So I slowed it down and went through it with him. He got so excited when the bear would speak in his low growly voice. After the story he went to the restroom. When he came back he stood at the door and did not want to come in. Did I mention this child is autistic? I found out from one of my staff that he was telling the story in the bathroom and then in the pod of classrooms. He was not going to come in until he was done telling the story. I love it! Isn't it great when a story does its work?"

Wendy learned this story from Sherry Norfolk, who told it, then had her teacher-students move through the story using their whole bodies and then retell it. Sherry's version of this Kiowa story, complete with her instructions for the movements, is found as "Grandmother Spider Brings the Light" in *More Ready-to-Tell Tales* by David Holt and Bill Mooney (August House, 2000). You can also read about how Sherry guided students to recreate the story through movement in *Literacy Development in the Story-telling Classroom* by Sherry Norfolk, Jane Stenson, and Diane Williams (Libraries Unlimited, 2009), pp. 123-129.

Telling a story one-on-one, as Wendy was doing with her telling of "Swim, Little Mouse," is another excellent way to share story with special needs listeners. That story incorporates a great deal of physical movement and repetitive language. For a text of "Swim Little Mouse" see www.margaretreadmacdonald.com. Click on Books. Click on Teaching with Story. Click on "Activities."

Even after the very first story with my students, they were participating and asking to do it again or for more stories. The more stories I told, the more involved they became. This in turn resulted in 100 percent participation by the students and a very high degree of comprehension of the story for recall and details. I found that each story provided not only a lesson to be learned, we could use that story for a real-life situation to discuss, and I could use each story multiple times in a number of ways to build comprehension.

— Kasey Clay, Covington Elementary, Covington, WA.

Using Technology

Three Kent, Washington teachers found storytelling brought amazing delight to their non-verbal preschool classes. The teachers prerecorded the tale's refrains onto each student's individual 'hit and listen' box. The student's aid helped position the child's hand over the box. For example, when the teacher paused in "Squeaky Door" saying, "the boy said…," the children all pushed their buttons, and throughout the room echoed the teacher's pre-recorded voice saying, "NO! Not ME!" Thus, the children were able to participate audibly within the stories she chose. The teachers recorded similar participation chants for each of the stories they wanted to use. These teachers were so pleased with the way storytelling en-ergized their classroom that they vowed to use this teaching technique from then on.

I was able to use storytelling as an assessment for one of my students with high verbal skill and low writing skills. He has an IEP which allows him accommodations for written work. I let him record his story [rather than writing it]. He is a very animated person and his written work would not have expressed his meaning in his story. [Storytelling] allowed him to put his own expression into it.

— Megan Garner, Grades 9-12 Art, Interlake High School, Bellevue, WA.

Repetition Is the Key

If you work in a pullout setting with students with severe learning needs, audience par-ticipation may look different or may need time to develop more gradually. Your audience will probably benefit from hearing the story more than one time. If they still like the story after a second time, they may want to hear it a third or a fourth time. Repetition enables students to learn the movements, chants, and phrases of the story. Often over time, students will find success and confidence working as a group playing with the story. With repeated telling, students also have multiple opportunities to hear *fine* language, develop linguistic skills, and bond together as a learning community.

Let's Look at Grandfather Bear

"Grandfather Bear" can be a perfect story to use with your special needs students. Tell it slowly and encourage students to join in the refrain, "I am SOOO hungry" with Grandfather Bear. Help your students act out the story and be sure to walk around and give everyone a reassuring stripe on the back at the story's end.

Try a Tale!

We have here two very simple tales with lots of participation. Have children who are able stand while you tell "Monkeys in the Rain." Encourage your students to make the motions with you and repeat the words after you.

Encourage children to croak for rain with the frogs and locusts in "Frog and Locust Bring the Rain." Have students who are able stand in place join in the frog/locust chorus—two "frogs" first, then four, then more and more until everyone is croaking.

Monkeys in the Rain
A Folktale from Brazil

[Tell your audience: "Say everything I say and do everything I do."]
The sun was shining! [Make a circle overhead with your arms.]
The monkeys said, "Let's play!" [Arms in the air!]
Hand-over-hand-over-hand—"It's fun!" [Swing through the trees.]
Hand-over-hand-over-hand—"It's fun!"
Hand-over-hand-over-hand—"It's fun!"

"Let's play chase!"
"Oo-oo-oo-oo-oo-oo" [Swinging and calling.]
"Caught you!" [Reach out as if to touch another monkey.]
"Oo-oo-oo-oo-oo-oo" [Swinging and calling.]
"Caught you!" [Reach out as if to touch another monkey.]

[Slap legs to simulate the patter of rain.]
"Rain! Rain! Rain! RAIN!"

"I'm cold…" [Hands protecting head from rain.]
"I'm wet"
"We should build a house!"
"Let's build a house."
"Tomorrow!"
"Tomorrow!"
"Tomorrow!"

Next day…
The sun was shining!
"Let's play!"
Hand-over-hand-over-hand—"It's fun!"
Hand-over-hand-over-hand—"It's fun!"
Hand-over-hand-over-hand—"It's fun!"

"Let's play chase!"

"Oo-oo-oo-oo-oo-oo" [Swinging and calling.]

"Caught you!" [Reach out as if to touch another monkey.]

"Oo-oo-oo-oo-oo-oo" [Swinging and calling.]

"Caught you!" [Reach out as if to touch another monkey.]

"Rain! Rain! Rain! RAIN!"

"I'm cold…" [Hands protecting on top of head.]

"I'm wet"

"We should build a house!"

"Let's build a house."

"Tomorrow!"

"Tomorrow!"

"Tomorrow!"

Next day…

The sun was shining! [Repeat all motions.]

"Let's play!"

Hand-over-hand-over-hand—"It's fun!"

Hand-over-hand-over-hand—"It's fun!"

Hand-over-hand-over-hand—"It's fun!"

"Let's play chase!"

"Oo-oo-oo-oo-oo-oo" [Swinging and calling.]

"Caught you!" [Reach out as if to touch another monkey.]

"Oo-oo-oo-oo-oo-oo" [Swinging and calling.]

"Caught you!" [Reach out as if to touch another monkey.]

And then…

"I'm cold…"

"I'm wet…"

"We should build a house!"

"Let's build a house!"

"Tomorrow."

"Tomorrow?" [Keep asking this until someone says "Today!" If necessary, you can ask, "Is tomorrow the right answer? When should we build our house?]

Don't be like the monkeys. Be like THIS person *[Point to person who gave the right answer.]* Build your house TODAY!

Source: *Five Minute Tales* by Margaret Read MacDonald (Atlanta: August House, 2007). This is *Motif J2171.2. Does not need roof when it is fair; cannot put it on when it rains.*

About Telling the Story: If your group is really rowdy or hard to control, drop the "caught you" part of the story, though you can usually draw them all back into the story by repeating the leg-slapping "Rain! Rain! Rain!"until all are focused again.

Extending the Tale

- Discuss procrastination.

- Draw or create a house for monkeys.

- Find the picture book *So Say the Little Monkeys* by Nancy Van Laan (Atheneum, 1998) and compare that tale with the one you just played with.

Frog and Locust Bring the Rain
A Hopi Story from the American Southwest

Here is a story in which everyone can participate. Divide the class into two halves, frogs and locusts. As you tell, you can bring the "frogs" or "locusts" to the front of the room to participate, or let them make their calls from their seats.

It didn't rain. It didn't rain.

Frog's puddle got smaller and smaller.

Frog tried to sing for rain.

[Ask one student to be frog and call with you]

"R-R-RAIN! "R-R-RAIN! "R-R-RAIN!

But he didn't sing very loud and the Rain God on top of the mountain did not hear.

Locust was so thirsty.

Locust tried to sing for rain.

[Ask one student to be locust and call with you.]

"r-r-rain! r-r-rain! r-r-rain!"

But she didn't sing very loud and the Rain God on top of the mountain did not hear.

Locust started to cry.
"eh...he...he...he..."

Frog heard someone crying.
"What is the matter, Locust?"
"If it doesn't rain, I will die," wailed Locust.
Then Frog started to cry too.
"If it doesn't rain I will die too!" wailed Frog.

Then Locust had an idea.
"Frog, if one person works alone, he can't do much.
But if people work together they can do things.
Let's both sing for rain together, Frog."

"I like that idea," said Frog. So both sang together.
[Both students help you call for rain now.]
"R-R-RAIN! "R-R-RAIN! "R-R-RAIN! "r-r-rain! r-r-rain! r-r-rain!"

But they didn't sing very loud and the Rain God on top of the mountain did not hear.

But it WAS loud enough to reach the next puddle. The frogs living there heard.
So they began to call too.
[Ask one or two more students to join in]
"R-R-RAIN! "R-R-RAIN! "R-R-RAIN!

And it WAS loud enough to reach the next bush.
The locusts there heard. They began to call too.
[Ask one or two more students to join as locusts.]
"r-r-rain! r-r-rain! r-r-rain!"

But it wasn't loud enough. And the Rain God on top of the mountain did not hear.

Repeat this several times, adding in a few frogs and locusts each time, until the entire class is calling for rain.

Now all the frogs were singing. All the locusts were singing.
The sound went clear to the top of the mountain!

The Rain God heard it! And the wind began to blow. *[Blow!]*
The lightning began to flash. *[Strike glancing blows, sliding one hand against the other to simulate lightning.]*
The thunder roared. *[Clap your hands loudly to simulate thunder.]*
And the rain fell. *[Pattering on knees with hands]*

Today the Hopi say that if one person's field is too dry,
He doesn't go off and sing by himself.
ALL of the people gather together.
With one heart they dance. And with one voice they sing.
And the Rain God sends down rain.

Source: *Earth Care: World Folktales to Talk About* by Margaret Read MacDonald (Atlanta: August House, 2005). Simplified from a tale by Joe Hayes in *Here Comes the Storyteller*. Cinco Puntos Press, 1996, p. 8-13. Read the full version at: www.cincopuntos.com/files/productspdf_43.pdf. *Motif A2426.4.1.2.2 In drought Rain Spirit responds when frogs dig deep holes and all croak.*

Extending the Tale

- Learn about the Hopi.

- Study weather patterns in the Southwest.

- Find soundtracks or videos of locusts singing.

- Find soundtracks or videos of frogs croaking.

- If other animals helped call for rain, what would this sound like?

- For a Spanish version of the story see: www.margaretreadmacdonald.com.

Ready…Set…Tell!

Choose a story from this book that has simple language, repetition, and is direct in its plot, perhaps "The Squeaky Door" or "Koala and Tree Kangaroo." Share the story slowly, using lots of physical actions. Encourage your students to repeat phrases with you and to use their bodies to copy your actions. Tell the story again tomorrow, and the next day!

Part Two:
Making Story Your Own

Chapter 10: Fixing a Tale in Your Mind— One Quick Way to Learn a Story

"I will not fail," the water bearer's daughter vowed. "But worse than failing is not to try at all. For then there can be no hope of success."
— Cameron Dokey, *The Storyteller's Daughter: A Retelling of "The Arabian Nights"*

So how do you learn all these wonderful stories we are suggesting you share with your students? Learning a story is not difficult at all. You tell stories every day without even realizing it. You tell the story of the traffic jam you experienced on the way to work. You tell the story of the adorable thing your little daughter did last night in the park. You "know" these stories because you have lived them. You can treat the folktale the same way. Read it over a few times. Read it aloud several times. Enter the story emotionally and "live" it. Walk yourself through the story and feel the emotion of the tale from the perspective of each of the characters. Then just tell what happened. Do not try to memorize the exact words, just retell the story.

Here are our simple steps to learning a tale. You can learn a story in many ways, but this technique puts a new story in your head, ready to tell, in less than an hour.

1. Choose a story you really love. The story should be one that makes you exclaim, "I can't wait to tell this to my students!" Don't waste your time on stories that do not evoke this excitement in you.

2. Find a space where you can concentrate. Turn off your distracting devices and put the mobile phone on "silent."

3. Read the story aloud. Listen to your words as you read. One good way to learn a new story is to hear another teller sharing the tale. But since you have no one to tell this story to you, tell it out loud to yourself.

4. Read the story aloud again. This time, work on the oral interpretation of the tale. Where do you want to get loud? Where does a softer voice seem right? Where should you speed the telling? Or slow down? Pause for effect? Notice lush words in the text that you want to be sure to keep. Savor these as you speak them.

5. Decide exactly how you want to open and close your tale. The opening is crucial. This is the magical moment in which you bring your listeners into the tale. It should be re-

hearsed and polished. So plan exactly what you will say. It can be as simple as "Once upon a time…" Choose a phrase to lead the audience into your tale, "Grandfather Bear woke up. It was spring!" You also need a well-rehearsed phrase to bring your tale to a close. "The end" will serve or "And they lived happily ever after." Or, as in good old "Grandfather Bear," "When anyone sees your stripes, they will remember how kind you were to share with Grandfather Bear." Any ending is fine. You just need to know in advance exactly what you plan to say, so that you can exit the story gracefully.

6. If there are any key phrases or chants within your story that you want to use, be sure to memorize them. Mabela and her mouse friends sing, "When we are marching, we never look back. The cat is at the end. *FO FENG!*" Her father warns her "When you are out and about, keep your ears open and listen. When you speak, pay attention to what you are saying. If you have to move, MOVE FAST!" The rest of the story is just told in your own words. But these key phrases need to be committed to memory so that students can join in successfully.

7. Put the text down and try telling the story in your own words. You already know the first and last sentences and the key phrases. Just tell it through. If you forget something, check your text. Sometimes it is useful to photocopy the story and make notes to help you remember how you want to tell the tale.

8. Now try to tell the story all the way through from beginning to end without looking at your text.

9. Rehearse in a space where you can move around. Research has shown that you can learn more when you are standing. So stand to rehearse your tale. Move around the room as you rehearse. Leave your arms free to gesture, and throw your body into the telling. When telling to an audience, some tellers like to move around a lot. Others will want to sit quietly and hardly move at all. Either style is fine. But if you rehearse using lots of movement, your body will have a kinesthetic sense of the tale. This will help you remember the story when you share it later.

This whole process should take under an hour if you have chosen a short (five-minute or less) folktale that has repetition. All of the stories in this book should be learnable in less than an hour using this technique.

Different Learning Styles

Learning styles are different, and the way we perceive story is different. When Jen was a little girl, Margaret once asked Jen and her sister, Julie, what they "saw" when they heard a certain story. Jen began to describe in detail the interior of the cabin in the story. None of these details had ever been mentioned in the telling nor were they ever imagined by Margaret when she told the story. Julie, on the other hand, didn't say a word at first. She grabbed a pencil and began to draw feverishly. Only when she was drawing did the words come, "The bear went here…then here…then here. The girl went here…" To her the story was all about movement and action. Every child will interact with the stories they hear in a unique way.

Just as we think about how to make our lessons engaging for the learning styles of our students, be aware of your own! Some tellers find it useful to create a visual representation of the story during their learning process. This can be a story map or a simple cartoon of the tale's scenes. Other tellers like to make a recording and listen to it over and over. Some match movements to particular parts of the story to help remember the tale. Nat is a kinesthetic learner and finds it useful to practice stories while playing Frisbee in the park. He and Jen toss the Frisbee back and forth saying lines from the story they are trying to learn with each toss.

So, find your own way to internalize the tale. If imagining entire scenes helps, do that. If drawing a map of the story helps, use that method. Sing the tale, act it out—whatever it takes to fix the storyline in your memory. But DO NOT MEMORIZE! Memorization creates a static text and does not allow the story to flow and change as you and your listeners play with it.

Storytelling Rehearsal on the Go

Take advantage of the quiet moments in your life to go over the story in your mind:

- Tell it aloud as you shower in the morning.

- Take a walk and go over the story.

- Tell it aloud as you drive to work.

Remember you aren't trying to *perfect* the story. You are just trying to feel comfortable speaking it.

Hitting the "Save" Button

Once you like the way your story sounds—the way the telling feels—make a recording of yourself sharing it with an audience. Don't make a big deal of this. Just tuck an audio device down at your side, turn it on, and let it capture your telling. No one need even know that recording is taking place. But you have a record of the way you told the story. Next year, when that unit comes around again, you don't have to go looking for the tale text and remember how you told the story. Just turn on your audio device and there you are, telling it just the way you created it. This tactic of recording your tales is a time-saving way to keep your repertoire alive from year to year.

Sharing the Tale with an Audience

On the day you plan to tell the story for the first time, set aside a few minutes to go over the story once more. Speak the story out loud. Imagine your audience in front of you and pretend you are telling to them. Just go over the story once. Don't fret. Any way you tell will be just fine.

Telling the Tale

1. Gather the class with your eyes. Hold their eyes for a moment in silence. This is the pregnant pause before the story begins.

2. Attack the story strongly with your first well-rehearsed sentence. The confidence of this beginning lets the listeners know they are in good hands. They can relax and enjoy the story.

3. As you tell the story, watch your listeners. Focus on *communicating* this story to them. Storytelling is not about performing. It doesn't matter how you look, or stand, or sound, as long as you can be heard. Storytelling is about sharing. You want to place this great tale in their hearts. Storytelling should be a nurturing act. It is all about caring for your audience by offering them story.

4. Keep your voice strong enough so that everyone is hearing every word. This doesn't necessarily mean a loud level; a quiet voice can still be strong and carry to the back of the room. But be sure your voice is projecting to that furthest listener.

5. Close your tale with your strong, rehearsed ending. This technique gives a satisfying feel of closure to the event.

6. Pause at the end of the story to let the class come back from the story moment. Listeners enter a sort of story trance when they descend into the world of a story. They need time to emerge from that trance.

7. Tell the story again and again. The first time you tell the story it will feel shaky. But you will not tell the story just once. Your students will want to hear the story again. And again. And once the *other* second-grade class learns that you have stories to tell, you will be in demand to share stories around the school. Practice is what makes you

a good storyteller. So you will need to be brave at first and offer your storytelling to other classes. The more times you tell, the easier it will become, and the more deeply fixed in your memory the story will go.

OH NO, I Forgot!

Everyone forgets parts of a story from time to time—it even happens to professional tellers onstage. Here are a few tips for managing a forgetful moment:

- If you leave something important out during the telling, just say, "Oh did I tell you…?" and add the missing information.

- If you forget your train of thought entirely, keep a copy of the text on hand. You can say, "What happened next? I don't remember! Let's see!" And check your text. Then return to the story flow. Jen has had times when there was a story she'd love to share with her class, but didn't have time to learn the tale. She just placed the text in her lap and told as much as she could from memory, glancing down when there was a bit she was unsure about.

- Don't expect the hiccups to happen—just be prepared to relax and accept them without worry if they arrive. Laughing about our mistakes, being flexible, and moving on confidently can be important modeling for our students. And as teachers, we're required to be masters of improvisation every day!

Controlled Chaos

Another wonderful benefit to approaching storytelling as a teacher is that you already have audience management techniques under your belt. You'd like the kids to lean in and listen even more carefully during part of the story? Lower your volume. You'd like to get a response from everyone at once during a story? After taking a few individual responses, you might say, "Okay, now on the count of three, everyone whisper what else was swimming in the water." Controlling a crowd is an important storytelling skill and teachers have loads of practice doing it well.

Remember, it's okay to let the children playing with the story get a little wild. Jen and Nat had an experience recently when we were tandem-telling a story about a war between the Sandpipers and the Whales (*Surf War*, August House, 2009). Half of the students were acting as sea creatures and the other half were pretending to be birds. We've told this story many, many times together and in lots of different settings. On this particular day, with this particular group of students, everything went crazy! It was an explosion of sea creatures and birds. All of our usual management techniques failed us and we had to stop the story for a moment to regain control. We left that session feeling that we had completely failed the students and the story, that it was a complete disaster. Weeks and months later, however, students were still talking about how much they loved that story and how wonderful it had been to be the sea creatures. What had seemed like a disaster to us had actually been a success for the students. As a result, we learned that sometimes we need to open ourselves up to the silliness and embrace it. Our students will thank us for it!

Finding the Tale

Finding the right tale is half the journey in telling a story successfully. We have given you many tales to get you started. Begin with these and feel the joy of telling. Later you will want to find more tales to integrate into your instruction in a variety of ways. Larger public libraries and university libraries will have copies of indexes which allow you to search for stories by subject or title. You can search for tales about frogs, clouds, greed, Africa—whatever topic fits your needs. Look for these indexes:

> *The Storyteller's Sourcebook: A Subject, Title, and Motif-Index to Folklore Collections for Children* by Margaret Read MacDonald: Detroit: Neal Schuman/Gale Research, 1982.

> *The Storyteller's Sourcebook: A Subject, Title, and Motif-Index to Folklore Collections for Children, 1983-1999* by Margaret Read MacDonald and Brian Sturm, Detroit: Gale Research, 2001.

Folklorists classify folktales by Type and Motif numbers. These books index 766 folktale collections and 1179 picture books. You can look up your story by subject or title, or by motif number. We give motif numbers in this book for the stories we include. These indexes can help you locate additional versions of the stories you are using. You might want to compare versions and create your own tale from the many ways that story is told around the world.

Check the web. You can find stories on topics or additional versions of stories by a web search, but be careful! You will find many poorly written tales online. Anyone can post a story text without citing sources and with little regard for literary merit or tellability.

Ask your librarian. This is the quickest and surest way to find useful material. Both your school librarian and the children's librarian at your public library have deep knowledge of resources. Tell them the topics for which you need stories and they will point the way.

"How-To" Resources for Beginning Tellers

Below are our favorite books for beginning tellers. More books are listed in our bibliography on page 205.

Farrell, Catharine. *Storytelling: A Guide for Teachers*. New York: Scholastic, 1991. Easy to read comments about storytelling, as well as reflections to help you think about story. Eight simple story texts are included with suggestions for extending the stories in the classroom.

MacDonald, Margaret Read. *The Storyteller's Start-up Book: Finding, Learning, Performing, and Using Folktales*. Little Rock: August House, 1993. How-to-select, learn, and perform a folktale. You'll find advice on teaching with story and teaching others to tell, plus twelve easy-to-learn tales.

Sawyer, Ruth. *The Way of the Storyteller*. New York: Penguin, 1997. This 1942 classic offers inspirational discussions about storytelling from one of the profession's early greats.

Walsh, John. *The Art of Storytelling: Easy Steps to Presenting an Unforgettable Story*. Chicago: Moody, 2003. Christian educator, John Walsh, offers clear advice for the beginning teller.

Creating Personal Stories

Don't forget that students love to hear your own personal stories as well! You already know many engaging stories from your own life experiences. With a little thought, these can be shaped for telling to your students. Sharing a little of yourself delights your students and lets them know you better as a person—not just as their teacher. And these are stories you don't even have to learn—you already know them!

We give suggestions for shaping and sharing personal stories in Chapter 7. You can find advice there for telling your own personal story and for helping your students shape theirs. A useful getting-started book for those wanting to shape personal stories is *Telling Your Own Stories* by Donald Davis (Atlanta: August House, 1993).

I really connected with [the idea of] sharing something of yourself. I personally enjoy having a close relationship with my students and often tell personal stories to give them a laugh or teach them something I feel is important. Personal storytelling creates an atmosphere where the students and I get to know each other better and gives us a more personal bond beyond the student/teacher relationship.

— Vanessa Garrard, Choir, H.M. Jackson High School
and Gateway Middle School, Everett, WA.

Enjoy the Telling!

Once you have your tale ready to share, the most important thing to remember is to *enjoy* the story with your students. Children are extremely forgiving with us as tellers. They don't care if our delivery is perfect or we use incredible character voices. They just want to get lost in a good story!

Remember, there is no right way or wrong way to tell a story. There are as many different ways to tell a story as there are humans in the universe. Any way you tell the story is the *right* way. If you are playing with folktales, the folktale is *yours. You* are one of the *folk!* So just take the story, make it your own, and share it—right away!

Storyteller Joe Hayes says, "If you hear a story and want to keep it with you, you need to tell it before the sun goes down!"

Chapter 11: Happily Ever After— Becoming a Narrative Leader in Your School!

If stories come to you, care for them. And learn to give them away where they are needed. Sometimes a person needs a story more than food to stay alive.

— Barry Lopez, *Crow and Weasel*

You Are a Storyteller!

Congratulations! You are now ready to find the joy of storytelling in your classroom.

Now that you are a storyteller, be sure to let your entire school community profit from your tales. Listen for the curriculum focus of your colleagues in school. If you know a story that would enhance someone's unit, offer to share it with their students!

If you are collaborating with another class on a regular basis, storytelling can be something you offer to the partnership. Lead the classes in storytelling activities. Have your students share stories with your buddy class.

If your school holds regular assemblies, find a story that fits the theme and offer to share it. A short tale, such as "Two Goats on a Bridge," is fun to tell and energizes any group—no matter how large!

One reward of sharing your stories around the school is that other students will feel that they know you personally. You may find that you are a celebrity in the halls! This allows you to have connections with many students you might not otherwise know.

Another way to share story with your school is by letting your students share their tales with other classes. This brings a feeling of pride to your students, and makes *them* celebrities in the hall! You could even start a storytelling club and finish the year with a performance for parents.

And if interest in storytelling grows in your school, why not offer to give interested teachers or parents a mini-course in storytelling? Teach them to tell a few stories, using the same techniques you are using with your students. There can never be too much storytelling going on in a school. Let it spread!

Connect with Other Tellers

Your area will likely have local storytelling guilds with tellers eager to support you in your storytelling journey. You can probably find those listed on the website of the National Storytelling Network. NSN offers annual conferences, a quarterly journal, and a website useful to keep you in touch with the world of storytelling, www.storynet.org

Taking Part in the Storytelling Tradition

Storytelling is an essential part of our human existence. The earliest recorded evidence we have of the storytelling tradition are folktales that were written on cuneiform clay tablets around four thousand years ago. Margaret first discovered these in a book by Theodore H. Gaster, *The Oldest Stories in the World* (Beacon, 1952). She was surprised to discover that the ending of one story was not known, because the clay tablet had been broken and that part of the story was lost. But she already knew how the story ended. How is this possible? She had just read the same tale in a collection of Russian folktales. The attempt to preserve the story on a clay tablet failed, but because it was passed from teller to teller the same story is being shared today. Think how many humans have voiced that story to keep it alive for four thousand years. You are now part of that long, long chain of storytellers. Don't let your stories die—give them voice, give them life, pass them along to future generations.

The only thing you need now to be a storyteller is a really good story that you have told enough times to own and an audience to share that story with. And your reward? The pleasure of feeling the beautiful language of a much-loved story roll off your tongue, seeing the rapt faces of your audience, and knowing that you are lifting them out of their world for a moment and transporting them to a new and exciting realm. The sheer joy of it all!

The Gift of Joy

The act of sharing a story is a gift you give your students. When you put down the book and look directly into their eyes, you communicate from your heart to their hearts. This connection has the power to transform your learning community. Like a stone thrown in a pond, the impact of one story can send ripples through your classroom that will help shape your interactions and inform your conversations throughout the year. We hope that you share this gift freely with your students, that you use tales to travel across the Seven "C"s, and that you enjoy a lifetime of teaching with story.

A Final Tale

We'd like to leave you with one last story. "Lifting the Sky" illustrates the power of language and of community. It's a wonderful tale to use in all-school assemblies. We encourage you to share this story at a school gathering sometime soon. Get everyone to join with you as you push the sky up and shout, "Ya-HOW!" It's amazing what a school full of storytellers can accomplish together!

Lifting the Sky
Retold from an Upper Skagit story by Vi taq š blu Hilbert

The Creator was going there...going there...
His face was shining so brightly that no one could look on his face.
He had a whole basket full of languages.
The Creator was giving out these languages as he crossed this great land of ours.
"Here is a language for the Chippewa. Here is a language for the Seminole.
Here is a language for the Cherokee. A language for the Hopi. A language for the Sioux.
But when he arrived in the Pacific Northwest, he still had a whole basketful of languages left.
What to do? So he just dumped them all out!

Everybody got a different language.
The people in *this* valley spoke one language.
The people in *that* valley spoke a different language.
The people on *this* island spoke one language.
The people on *that* island spoke another language.
Nobody could communicate. Nobody could cooperate.

And in those days the Creator had made one mistake. He had left the sky too low.

Tall people were bumping their heads on it.
And some people were climbing up into the sky country before it was their time.
That could not be allowed.

So all the chiefs met together. How could they push up the sky?
If they had only one word that they all shared, they could do it. They could cooperate.
They decided on a word. Ya-HOW! That would mean, "Go ahead!"

With that one word they could cooperate.

All of the chiefs went home and taught that word to their people. "Ya-HOW!"

They told their people to all cut long poles to push on the sky.

And all together they pushed and shouted. "Ya-HOW!"

But they did not push hard enough.

"Everybody must put their back into this. Everybody must shout!"

"Ya-HOW!"

Still not hard enough. Not everybody is helping. "Everybody!"

"Ya-HOW!"

And because this is a Native American story, the magic number is not three …

The magic nunber is FOUR so one more time.

"All the shoulders. All voices. Cooperate!"

"Ya-HOW!"

And the sky flew up where it is today. You don't need to worry about bumping your head on the sky ever again.

And this shows what can happen…if we all share even one word…and cooperate.

"Ya-HOW!"

Source: "Lifting the Sky" is retold from Vi **taq š blu** Hilbert's version in *Peace Tales: World Folktales to Talk About* by Margaret Read MacDonald (August House, 1991), p. 82-85. This is a story from Vi's Upper Skagit elders, told originally in the Lushootseed language.

Part Three:
Standards, Research, and Resources

Chapter 12: Storytelling and the Common Core Standards

The power of stories is that they perform two tasks at the same time. They are very effective at communicating information in a memorable form, and they can orient the hearer's feelings about the information being communicated.

— Kieran Egan, *An Imaginative Approach to Teaching*

We know that quality teaching starts with being mindful of what we want students to know and to be able to do. Curricular documents differ in schools around the globe, but whether we're focused on "standards and benchmarks" or "learning outcomes" or "enduring understandings," the end result is the same. We need to plan with purpose and make sure that the learning engagements we design for our students each day are focused on these objectives.

Here again, storytelling proves to be an invaluable teaching tool. Anytime you take the time to share a story, you are automatically touching on a variety of language outcomes that are universal such as visualizing, predicting, and listening.

Take a story and then see how many standards and benchmarks you can link to that particular tale. It's amazing how many connections one quick tale can make to the important teaching and learning that is already taking place in your classroom!

Language Arts Common Core Standards That Can Be Supported by Oral Storytelling

Let's take a look at the Common Core Standards currently being implemented in the United States in the area of English Language Arts. For more detailed information go to: www.corestandards.org. Just reading quickly through the list of standards, you can see that storytelling strategies can easily be applied to help students reach the majority of these outcomes. Some of the standards actually require oral storytelling on the part of your students. And by selecting certain tales and tailoring your follow-up work, you can find stories with language that will help you teach toward any of these standards. We are noting standards here only for grades K-5, but a glance at standards for upper levels will show how storytelling can be used to fulfill standards throughout the age ranges. And a look through your state standards for social studies, math, science, health and fitness, environmental studies, and the arts will reveal many more places to use story to meet standards.

Emphasis on Folktales

The use of folktales is required by some of the core standards. This gives you an excellent opportunity for oral storytelling. For example:

Grade 2:
RL.2.9 Compare and contrast two or more versions of the same story (e.g., Cinderella stories) by different authors from different cultures.

Grade 3:
RL. 3.2 Recount stories, including fables, folktales, and myths from diverse cultures; determine the central message, lesson or moral and explain how it is conveyed through key details in the text.

Grade 4:
RL. 4.9 Compare and contrast the treatment of themes and topics (e.g., opposition of good and evil) and patterns of events (e.g., the quest) in stories, myths, and traditional literature from different cultures.

In addition, storytelling is an excellent vehicle to address the many other standards that examine text. When the story is told first, the group experiences the joy of the story. Later discussion of textual details such as setting, plot, characterization, phraseology, and point of view are easier because the group has shared in the told story.

Reading Standards for Literature K–5

Kindergarten:
RL. K.2 With prompting and support, retell familiar stories, including key details.

RL. K.3 With prompting and support, identify familiar characters, settings, and major events in a story.

RL. K.9 With prompting and support, compare and contrast the adventures and experiences of characters in familiar stories.

Grade 1:

RL. 1.2 Retell stories, including key details, and demonstrate understanding of their central message or lesson.

RL. 1.3 Describe characters, settings, and major events in a story, using key details.

RL. 1.4 Identify words and phrases in stories or poems that suggest feelings or appeal to the senses.

RL. 1.9 Compare and contrast the adventures and experiences of characters in stories.

Grade 2:

RL. 2.2 Recount stories, including fables and folktales from diverse cultures, and determine their central message, lesson, or moral.

RL. 2.4 Describe how words and phrases (e.g., regular beats, alliteration, rhymes and repeated lines) supply rhythm and meaning in a story, poem, or song.

RL. 2.5 Describe the overall structure of a story, including describing how the beginning introduces the story and the ending concludes the action.

RL. 2.6 Acknowledge difference in the points of view of characters.

RL. 2.9 Compare and contrast two or more versions of the same story (e.g., Cinderella stories) by different authors from different cultures.

Grade 3:

RL. 3.2 Recount stories, including fables, folktales, and myths from diverse cultures; determine the central message, lesson or moral and explain how it is conveyed through key details in the text.

RL 3.3 Describe characters in a story (e.g., their traits, motivations, or feelings) and explain how their actions contribute to the sequence of events.

RL. 3.6 Distinguish their own point of view from that of the narrator or those of the characters.

Grade 4:

RL. 4.2 Determine a theme of a story, drama, or poem from details in the text; summarize the text.

RL. 4.3 Describe in depth a character, setting, or event in a story or drama, drawing on specific details in the text (e.g., a character's thoughts, words, or actions).

RL 4.4 Determine the meaning of words and phrases as they are used in a text, including those that allude to significant characters found in mythology (e.g., Herculean).

RL. 4.6 Compare and contrast the point of view from which different stories are narrated, including the difference between first-and-third-person narrations.

RL. 4.9 Compare and contrast the treatment of similar themes and topics (e.g., opposition of good and evil) and patterns of events (e.g., the quest) in stories, myths, and traditional literature from different cultures.

Grade 5:

RL. 5.2 Determine a theme of a story, drama, or poem from details in the text, including how characters in a story or drama respond to challenges or how the speaker in a poem reflects upon a topic; summarize the text.

RL. 5.3 Compare and contrast two or more characters, settings, or events in a story or drama, drawing on specific details in the text (e.g., how characters interact).

RL. 5.5 Explain how a series of chapters, scenes, or stanzas fit together to provide the overall structure of a particular story, drama, or poem.

RL. 5.6 Describe how a narrator's or speaker's point of view influences how events are described.

RL. 5.7 Analyze how the visual and multimedia elements contribute to the meaning, tone, or beauty of a text (e.g., a graphic novel, multimedia presentation of fiction, folktale, myth, [or] poem).

RL. 5.9 Compare and contrast stories in the same genre (e.g., mysteries and adventure stories) on their approaches to similar themes and topics.

Speaking and Listening Standards K–5

Kindergarten:

SL. K.2 Confirm understanding of a text read aloud or information presented orally or through other media by asking and answering questions about key details and requesting clarification, if something is not understood.

SL. K.4 Describe familiar people, places, things, and events and, with prompting and support, provide additional detail.

SL. K.6 Speak audibly and express thoughts, feelings, and ideas clearly.

Grade 1:

SL. 1.2 Ask and answer questions about key details in a text read-aloud or information presented orally or through other media.

SL. 1.4 Describe people, places, things, and events with relevant details expressing ideas and feelings clearly.

Grade 2:

SL. 2.2 Recount or describe key ideas or details from a text read aloud or information presented orally or through other media.

SL. 2.4 Tell a story or recount an experience with appropriate facts and relevant, descriptive details, speaking audibly in coherent sentences.

SL. 2.5 Create audio recordings of stories or poems; add drawings or other visual displays to stories or recounts of experiences, when appropriate to clarify ideas, thoughts, and feelings.

Grade 3:

SL. 3.4 Report on a topic or text, tell a story, or recount an experience in an organized manner, using appropriate facts and relevant, descriptive details to support main ideas or themes; speak clearly at an understandable pace.

SL. 3.5 Create engaging audio recordings of stories or poems that demonstrate fluid reading at an understandable pace; add visual displays, when appropriate to emphasize or enhance certain facts or details.

SL. 3.6 Speak in complete sentences, when appropriate to task and situation, in order to provide requested detail or clarification.

Grade 4:

SL. 4.2 Paraphrase portions of a text read aloud or information presented in diverse media and formats, including visually, quantitatively, and orally.

SL. 4.4 Report on a topic or text, tell a story, or recount an experience in an organized manner, using appropriate facts and relevant, descriptive details to support main ideas or themes; speak clearly at an understandable pace.

SL. 4.5 Add audio recordings and visual displays to presentations, when appropriate to enhance the development of main ideas or themes.

SL 4.6 Differentiate between contexts that call for formal English (e.g., presenting ideas) and situations where informal discourse is appropriate (e.g., small-group discussion); use formal English when appropriate to task and situation.

Grade 5:

SL. 5.2 Summarize a written text read aloud or information presented in diverse media and formats, including visually, quantitatively, and orally.

SL. 5.5 Include multimedia components (e.g. graphics, sound, and visual displays) in presentations, when appropriate to enhance the development of main ideas or themes.

Sl. 5.6 Adapt speech to a variety of contexts and tasks using formal English when appropriate to task and situation.

Writing Standards K–5

Kindergarten:

W.K.3 Use a combination of drawing, dictating, and writing to narrate a single event or several loosely linked events, tell about the events in the order in which they occurred, and provide a reaction to what happened.

W.K.5 With guidance and support from adults, respond to questions and suggestions from peers and add details to strengthen writing as needed.

Grade 1:

W.1.3 Write narratives in which they recount two or more appropriately sequenced events, include some details regarding what happened, use temporal words to signal event order, and provide some sense of closure.

W.1.5 With guidance and support from adults, focus on a topic, respond to questions and suggestions from peers, and add details to strengthen writing as needed.

Grade 2:

W.2.3 Write narratives in which they recount a well-elaborated event or short sequence of events, include details to describe actions, thoughts, and feelings, use temporal words to signal event order, and provide a sense of closure.

W.2.5 With guidance and support from adults and peers, focus on a topic and strengthen writing as needed by revising and editing.

Grade 3:

W.3.3 Write narratives to develop real or imagined experiences or events using effective technique, descriptive details, and clear event sequences.

W.3.5 With guidance and support from peers and adults, develop and strengthen writing as needed by planning, revising, and editing.

Grade 4:

W.4.3 Write narratives to develop real or imagined experiences or events using effective technique, descriptive details, and clear event sequences.

W.4.5 With guidance and support from peers and adults, develop and strengthen writing as needed by planning, revising, and editing.

Grade 5:

W.5.3 Write narratives to develop real or imagined experiences or events using effective technique, descriptive details, and clear event sequences.

W.5.5 With guidance and support from peers and adults, develop and strengthen writing as needed by planning, revising, editing, rewriting, or trying a new approach.

Language Standards K–5

Kindergarten:

L. K.1 Demonstrate command of the conventions of Standard English grammar and usage when writing or speaking.

L. K.5 With guidance and support from adults, explore word relationships and nuances in word meanings.

Grade 1:

L. 1.1 Demonstrate command of the conventions of Standard English grammar and usage when writing or speaking.

L. 1.5 With guidance and support from adults, demonstrate understanding of figurative language, word relationships, and nuances in word meanings.

Grade 2:

L. 2.1 Demonstrate command of the conventions of Standard English grammar and usage when writing or speaking.

L. 2.3 Use knowledge of language and its conventions when writing, speaking, reading, or listening. Compare formal and informal uses of English.

L. 2.5 Demonstrate understanding of figurative language, word relationships, and nuances in word meanings.

L. 2.6 Use words and phrases acquired through conversations, reading and being read to, and responding to texts, including using adjectives and adverbs to describe (e.g., *When other kids are happy that makes me happy*).

Grade 3:

L. 3.1 Demonstrate command of the conventions of Standard English grammar and usage when writing or speaking.

L. 3.3 Use knowledge of language and its conventions when writing, speaking, reading, or listening. Choose words and phrases for effect. Recognize and observe differences between the conventions of spoken and written Standard English.

L. 3.5 Demonstrate understanding of figurative language, word relationships, and nuances in word meanings.

L. 3.6 Acquire and use accurately grade-appropriate conversational, general academic, and domain-specific words and phrases, including those that signal spatial and temporal relationships (e.g., *After dinner that night we went looking for them*).

Grade 4:

L. 4.3 Use knowledge of language and its conventions when writing, speaking, reading, or listening.

L. 4.5 Demonstrate understanding of figurative language, word relationships, and nuances in word meanings.

Grade 5:

L. 5.1 Observe conventions of grammar and usage when writing or speaking.

L. 5.3 Use knowledge of language and its conventions when writing, speaking, reading, or listening.

L. 5.4 Expand, combine, and reduce sentences for meaning, reader/listener interest, and style. Compare and contrast the varieties of English (e.g., *dialects, registers*) used in stories, dramas, or poems.

L. 5.5 Demonstrate understanding of figurative language, word relationships, and nuances in word meanings.

The Youth, Educators, and Storytellers Alliance (YES) special interest group of the National Storytelling Network has produced a list of suggested story activities to teach to these standards. You can download this and join their group at www.storynet.com]

Spot the Standard!

Take five minutes to look at your own curricular documents. Which benchmarks could storytelling strategies in the classroom help your students meet? How many can you find? Now, take a story from this book and play "Spot the Standard"—how can you use that one story to meet your desired outcomes? Try it today!

Chapter 13: Research Supports Storytelling in the Classroom

A necessary part of our intelligence is on the line as the oral tradition becomes less and less important. There was a time throughout our land when it was common for stories to be told and retold, a most valuable exercise, for the story retold is the story reexamined over and over again at different levels of intellectual and emotional growth.

— West Jackson, *Becoming a Native to This Place*

"Research says…" we've all heard those words many times. We always want to make sure our instructional practices are grounded in current research. So what does the research say about storytelling?

Kendall Haven, a storyteller and educator, provides an in-depth look at research on the importance of story in his 2007 book *Story Proof: The Science Behind the Startling Power of Story.* In *Story Proof*, Haven examined 350 research studies from 15 different fields of science and tells us that each of these studies concluded that, "stories are an effective and efficient vehicle for teaching, for motivating, and for the general communication of factual information, concepts, and tacit information." Haven cites a range of studies in the field of neural science that show how our brains organize information with the help of neural maps. These studies suggest that we are literally hard-wired for story.

Since the brain is wired for story, storytelling is an especially useful way to fasten information in memory. Eric Jensen's *Teaching with the Brain in Mind* (Association for Supervision and Curriculum Development, 1998) explains how memories are stored in various locations in the brain. The more locations a memory is stored in, the greater the likelihood that the memory will be retained. He says that storytelling is particularly useful because it connects content with emotion. When students learn something in the context of a story that engages them emotionally, they are more likely to be able to access that learning in the future. He also talks about the power of creating a narrative when key items need to be remembered. If you make up a story to help fix a list of items in your mind, he says, "It will supply a meaningful context for the items, and the plot provides an associative thread of ideas so that one triggers the next." (p.112).

Some current experts in education would like to put storytelling at the heart of all teaching. Kieran Egan, a professor at Simon Fraser University in British Columbia, suggests that all curricula should be based on storytelling. Professor Egan argues that students are capable of abstract thinking much earlier than anyone gives them credit for and that stories can help students think "out of the box" and access concepts that might be considered beyond them in a conventional setting. Stories provide the scaffolding for students to explore sophisticated topics in depth. Read his views in *Teaching as Storytelling: An Alternative Approach to Teaching and Curriculum in the Elementary School* (University of Chicago Press, 1986) and *An Imaginative Approach to Teaching* (Josey-Bass, 2005).

Kendal Haven has expressed surprise that even when research clearly shows the effectiveness of story, schools still have not realized the potential of storytelling as a teaching technique. He points out that the business world, in contrast, has recognized the value of storytelling and in recent years many businesses have begun to make storytelling an increasingly integral part of their corporate culture and a critical component in their advertising campaigns. (*Storytelling Magazine* May/June 2008).

We wish there were more large-scale quantitative studies that focused specifically on storytelling in the classroom and provided well-documented proof that storytelling works wonders. We know from our own use of story that it does and we've identified some smaller-scale studies that offer support for our position. Many anecdotal papers have been published suggesting that the use of storytelling in the classroom improves learning and builds community. This has certainly been our experience in our own classrooms and in those of our colleagues. Story is also an unusually strong way to effect changes in attitudes, as some of the research below shows. Here is a brief sample of research studies that have examined the effects of storytelling on student learning and that have direct implications for teaching and learning in our classrooms.

Effects of Storytelling on Vocabulary

1987: Froyen, Gail. "The effects of Storytelling Experiences on Vocabulary Skills of Second-Grade Students." Master of Arts research paper, Library Science Department, University of Northern Iowa. Second-grade students at Lowell School, Waterloo, Iowa, were taught storytelling techniques. Then they practiced and performed stories, working for 35-40 minutes each week for six months. This was a lunchtime project in which 43 students took part. The students, divided into groups of 8 or 9, were given Iowa tests of basic skills both pre- and post-project. Their scores increased significantly beyond what would have been expected.

Effects of Storytelling on Reading Comprehension

1998: Susan Trostle and Sandy Jean Hicks, "The Effects of Storytelling versus Story Reading on Comprehension and Vocabulary Knowledge of British Primary School Children" in *Reading Improvement*, v. 35 n.3 p.127-36, Fall 1998. Thirty-two primary children who witnessed stories being told scored higher on comprehension/vocabulary measures than a group who listened to stories read aloud.

Effects of Storytelling on Attitudes Toward Subject Matter

2006: Julia E. Watts. Benefits of Storytelling Methodologies in Fourth-and Fifth-Grade Historical Instruction. Thesis, Department of Curriculum and Instruction, East Tennessee State University, May, 2006. Two hundred twenty-eight fourth- and fifth-grade students in a Southern Indiana elementary school participated in the study in which half of the students listened to and participated in oral narratives during their lessons and half were taught by traditional lecture and note-taking instruction. A History Affinity Scale pre-and post-study test showed significant increase in the storytelling group. No changes were shown in the control group.

2005: Margaret B. Meyers. "Telling the Stars: A Quantitative Approach to Assessing the Use of Folk Tales in Science Education." Thesis, Department of Curriculum and Instruction, East Tennessee State University, December, 2005. Thirty-five hundred students in eight locations in the U.S. were taught scientific concepts about the stars by pairing stories viewed via video of teller Lynn Moroney with science information. A significant increase in positive attitude toward Science was found.

Effects of Storytelling on Memory

1995: Oaks, Tommy Dale. "Storytelling: A Natural Mnemonic: A study of a storytelling teaching method to positively influence student recall of instruction." Ph.D. dissertation, University of Tennessee, 1995. One hundred fourteen college students in Instructional Media and Technology courses were divided into two groups. One group was taught via storytelling techniques, the other with traditional methods. A pre-study test, a post-study test done immediately after instruction, and a test given three and five weeks following instruction all showed significantly greater gains in recall by the storytelling group over the control group.

1991: Smith, Ward William. "The effects of story presentation strategies on story recall and understanding of fourth graders with different information processing styles." Ed.D. dissertation, United States International University, 1991. Two hundred twenty-two fourth graders were tested to determine their learning styles. Students experienced a story either through storytelling, hearing the teacher read aloud, or independent reading. They were given a multiple-choice test-to-test short-term memory and a story-mapping activity to test long-term memory. Students, regardless of their learning styles (learning-sequential, integrated processors, or holistic-global) had better comprehension when experiencing the story through oral storytelling.

Effects of Storytelling on Creativity

1993: Finnerty, Joyce Carol Powell. "Instruction, imagery, and inference: The effects of three instructional methods on inferential comprehension of elementary children." Ed. D. dissertation, University of Virginia, 1993. During the study, 131 second-grade students were given creativity pre and post-tests. (Thinking Creatively in Action and Movement and Early Inventory Pre-literacy). A storytelling group, a story-reading group, and a control group were used. Both reading-aloud and storytelling groups showed statistically higher creativity scores, but the storytelling group's scores were highest. The increase in creativity scores was especially strong for the lower-socioeconomic students.

Effect of Storytelling on Writing

2006: Whitman, Nathaniel. "A Study of Storytelling's Effect on Primary (7-9 Year old) Writing." M.Ed. Thesis, University of Western Australia, 2006. Hong Kong International School second graders were given writing prompts. The first week they were given a prompt and then began to write immediately. A week later, after a different prompt, they were given a chance to tell their story to a partner before writing. The writing produced after storytelling was used as a pre-writing exercise showed more sophisticated sentence structure, a higher degree of organization, and stronger word choice in their final, written work.

1994: Gloria Jean Gebracht. "The Effect of Storytelling on the Narrative Writing of Third-Grade Students." Ph.D. Dissertation, Indiana University of Pennsylvania, 1994. Ninety-four third-grade students in four classes were given pre-and post-tests for writing skills. After listening to stories, significant gains were made in story composition and in oral storytelling skills. Greatest effect was had on the below-average readers.

Storytelling with Special Education

1980: Fuller, Renee. "STORY TIME: MIND" in OMNI, June, 1980, p.22, 119. Psychologist working with severely brain-damaged children with IQs of 20 and 30 found they were "suddenly able to gain reading comprehension because they were fed stories instead of a disjointed series of facts." She suggests that story comprehension is so basic that it survives severe neurological damage.

Chapter 14: Resources to Take You Further

The destiny of the world is determined less by the battles that are lost and won than by the stories it loves and believes in.

— Harold Clarke Goddard, *The Meaning of Shakespeare*

In preparing this book, we examined over 250 items dealing with storytelling and education. The following list is a selective bibliography of the books we think will be the most helpful resources for a beginning teacher-teller.

Barton, Bob, and David Booth. *Story Works: How Teachers Can Use Shared Stories in the New Curriculum*. Markham, Ontario: Pembroke, 2000. New edition of *Stories in the Classroom*. Two Canadian teachers stress building a story community where all can share and all can listen. Includes anecdotes and advice.

Brand, Susan Trostle, and Jeanne M. Donato, *Storytelling in Emergent Literacy: Fostering Multiple Intelligences*. Albany, NY: Delmar/Thomson Learning, 2001. There are chapters on benefits of storytelling, the use of storytelling to foster emergent literacy, and how to tell. The rest of book suggests stories and multiple intelligence activities to accompany each month of the year. Howard Gardner's multiple intelligences paradigm is used as a model. Included are story texts, chants, and puppet scripts.

Collins, Rives, and Pamela J. Cooper. *The Power of Story: Teaching Through Storytelling*. Long Grove, Ill: Waveland Press, Inc., 1997, 2nd ed, first titled *Look What Happened to Frog*. Includes information on selecting, learning, telling, and dramatizing tales, as well as many activities for classroom storytelling groups and interviews with several tellers.

De Las Casas, Dianne. *Tell Along Tales! Playing with Participation Stories*. Westport, CT: Libraries Unlimited, 2011. Good advice on using participation in storytelling, plus several retellings of simple folktales with lots of participation added by the author.

De Vos, Gail: *Storytelling for Young Adults: Techniques and Treasury*. Englewood, CO: Libraries Unlimited, 1991. Brief advice for telling to teens, and many suggestions of tales the author has found useful.

Farrell, Catharine. *Storytelling: A Guide for Teachers*. New York: Scholastic, 1991. Easy to read comments about storytelling, and suggestions to encourage reflection about story, as well as eight simple story texts with suggestions for extending them in the classroom.

Gillard, Marni. *Storyteller, Storyteacher: Discovering the Power of Storytelling for Teaching and Living*. York, Maine: Stenhouse Publishers, 1996. With advice from a Middle School teacher who encourages her students to tell, this book is especially useful for its thoughts on telling personal stories.

Greene, Ellin, and Janice del Negro. *Storytelling: Art and Technique*. 4th ed. Santa Barbara, CA: Libraries Unlimited, 2010. This 465 page book is designed for the public library children's librarian but has a great deal of information for the beginning storyteller. Especially useful are answers to frequently asked questions, extensive bibliographies, and website connections.

Hamilton, Martha, and Mitch Weiss. *Children Tell Stories: Teaching and Using Storytelling in the Classroom*. 2nd ed. Katonah, New York: Richard C. Owen, 2005. Everything you need to know to teach your students to tell. Includes a DVD with student storytellers. See also the authors' other collections of simple texts for student tellers.

Haven, Kendall. *Super Simple Storytelling: A Can-Do Guide for Every Classroom, Every Day*. Greenwood, CO: Libraries Unlimited, 2000. Focuses on how to learn and perform, as well as using storytelling in the curriculum. Includes many activities for student storytelling groups.

_____. *Story Proof: The Science Behind the Startling Power of Story*. Westport, CT: Libraries Unlimited, 2007. A review of the research to 2007 on use of story in the classroom.

_____. *Write Right! Creative Writing Using Storytelling Techniques*. Englewood, CO: Libraries Unlimited, 1999. Creative writing and storytelling ideas to stimulate student writing.

Hayes, Joe. *Here Comes the Storyteller*. El Paso, TX: Cinco Puntos, 1996. Nine tellable tales are featured, with photos of the author in action telling the tales and his comments about the telling. Great tales, easy to tell. For free download see: www.cincopuntos.com/files/productspdf_43.pdf.

Lipke, Barbara. *Figures, Facts & Fables: Telling Tales in Science and Math*. Portsmouth, N.H.: Heinemann, 1996. Suggestions from a teacher-teller for using story across the curriculum.

Lipman, Doug. *Improving Your Storytelling: Beyond the Basics for All Who Tell in Work or Play*. Little Rock: August House, 1999. For the more advanced teller. Useful for those developing personal stories for adult audiences, this book discusses use of a story buddy to help shape your material. There are chapters on imagery, kinesthetic tension, voice, and attention to audience.

MacDonald, Margaret Read. *The Parent's Guide to Storytelling*. Little Rock: August House, 2001. Easy-to-tell tales for pre-school and primary.

_____. *Shake-it-up Tales! Stories to Sing, Dance, Drum, and Act Out*. Atlanta: August House, 2000. Easy-to-tell stories from around the world, including chanting, singing, dancing and drumming tales. Plus stories with improvisational slots, riddle tales, tandem tales, story-theater, and suggestions for incorporating audience members onstage, and dramatizing tales with the entire group in movement. All are arranged for easy learning, with tips for telling.

_____. *Tell the World: Storytelling Across Language Barriers*. Westport, CT: Libraries Unlimited, 2008. Provides advice from the author and 41 other tellers on telling stories through translation with descriptions of several different storytelling techniques.

_____. *Twenty Tellable Tales: Audience Participation Folktales for the Beginning Storyteller*. Chicago: American Library Association, 2004. A collection of surefire, easy-to-learn tales.

Mooney, Bill, and David Holt. *The Storyteller's Guide: Storytellers Share Advice for the Classroom, Boardroom, Showroom, Podium, Pulpit, and Center Stage*. Little Rock: August House, 1996. Offers bits of advice from many professional tellers on finding the right story, shaping a story, creating your own personal story, and much more.

National Storytelling Association, *Tales as Tools. The Power of Story in the Classroom*. Jonesborough, TN: National Storytelling Press, 1994. Chapters on using storytelling in Language Arts, History, Science, Math, Healing, Peace and the Environment. Includes articles by professional tellers and teachers.

Norfolk, Bobby, and Sherry Norfolk. *The Moral of the Story: Folktales for Character Development*. Little Rock: August House, 1999. Presents twelve tales with notes on their use and discussion of the role of storytelling in character education.

Norfolk, Sherry, Jane Stenson, and Diane Williams, editors. *The Storytelling Classroom: Applications Across the Curriculum*. Westport, CT: Libraries Unlimited, 2006. Classroom uses for 50 stories submitted by professional storytellers and teachers. Pre-school to Grade 8.

_____. *Literacy Development in the Storytelling Classroom*. Westport, CT: Libraries Unlimited, 2009. Suggestions for using 58 stories in the classroom that were submitted by professional storytellers and teachers. Pre-school to Gr 8.

Norfolk, Sherry, and Jane Stenson, editors. *Social Studies in the Storytelling Classroom: Exploring Our Cultural Voices and Perspectives*. Little Rock: Parkhurst Brothers Publishing, 2012.

Paley, Vivian Gussin. *The Boy Who Would Be a Helicopter*. Cambridge: Harvard University Press, 1990. This Chicago pre-school teacher lets her children dictate a story of their imagining to her, then she reads it aloud to the class and the child directs a dramatization of the story. Other books by this author include: *The Kindness of*

Children (Harvard University Press, 2000), and *The Girl with the Brown Crayon* (Harvard University Press, 1998).

Pearmain, Elisa Davy. *Once Upon a Time: Storytelling to Teach Character and Prevent Bullying. Lessons from 99 Multicultural Folk Tales for Grades K-8.* Greensboro, NC: Character Development Group, 2006. All 99 tales deal with various character traits and include follow-up activities. Also has info on how to learn and tell stories.

Rubright, Lynn. *Beyond the Beanstalk: Interdisciplinary Learning through Storytelling.* Portsmouth, NH: Heinemann. 1996. Chapters on specific innovative uses this teacher has made of story in the classroom, including creation of new stories using a "story-weaving" technique, and extension into all areas of study, including math.

Rubinstein, Robert E. *Curtains Up! Theatre Games and Storytelling.* Golden, CO: Fulcrum, 2000. Theatre games to warm up student storytellers, including one chapter on training student storytellers.

Sawyer, Ruth. *The Way of the Storyteller.* New York: Penguin, 1976. A must-read for the beautiful way Sawyer speaks of storytelling. The eleven tales, however, are a bit difficult for beginning tellers.

Stanley, Nile, and Brett Dillingham, *Performance Literacy through Storytelling.* Gainesville, FL: Maupin House, 2009. See this book for its useful chapter on digital telling.

Sierra, Judy and Robert Kaminski. *Twice Upon a Time: Stories to Tell, Retell, Act Out, and Write About.* Bronx: H.W. Wilson, 1989. Twenty-one tellable folktales with suggested activities for retelling, dramatizing, and writing.

Strauss, Kevin. *Tales with Tails: Storytelling the Wonders of the Natural World.* Westport, CT: Libraries Unlimited, 2006. Offers ideas for using stories in environmental education. Includes a list of stories with sources.

Walsh, John. *The Art of Storytelling: Easy Steps to Presenting an Unforgettable Story.* Chicago: Moody, 2003. Religious educator, John Walsh, offers clear advice for the beginning teller.

Winston, Linda. *Keepsakes: Using Family Stories in Elementary Classrooms.* Portsmouth, N.H.: Heinemann, 1997. Ideas for encouraging students to write and retell family stories, as well as tips on having family members visit school to share stories, interviews with elders, use of family recipes and photos. This is especially useful as an integrating activity for immigrant families.

Web Connections

Many websites contain useful information for teachers wishing to use story in the classroom. There are a few listed below and you will find links to many more as you explore these sites.

www.storynet.org. Connect to the wider world of US storytellers through the National Storytelling Network. That group has special interest groups on many topics, including Environmental Storytelling; Healing Story Alliance; and Youth, Educators and Storytelling Alliance. You will find links to many resources at this website.

www.youthstorytelling.com. Website of Kevin Cordi. Information and links to articles about teaching kids to tell stories.

www.pitt.edu/~dash/folktexts.html. Website prepared by D. L. Ashliman offers full texts of numerous folktale classics. Good source to find texts for variants of classic folktales. Seventeen Beauty and the Beast tales are given, for example.

www.storynet-advocacy.org/edu/how-to. Links to articles and studies about storytelling in schools.

www.artofstorytellingshow.com. Interviews with storytellers on many topics. Site maintained by Eric Wolf.

www.storyteller.net. Articles about telling, interviews with tellers, and audio of some tellers. Site is maintained by Sean Buvala.

Index

Acknowledgements

We are grateful to our many talented colleagues around the world, both teachers and storytellers, who have shared their enthusiasm and ideas for using storytelling in the classroom with us over the years. Their collective wisdom has shaped this book. We give special thanks to Margaret Lippert, Jon Whitzman, Megan Chadwick, and Jan Otter for reviewing the book in its final stages. Our heartfelt appreciation goes to our publisher, Steve Floyd, for believing in the value of this project and to our editor, Judy O'Malley for helping us rein in our collective use of the dreaded exclamation mark! Finally, we want to thank the members of our extended family who showed patience and support as our dinner conversations shifted time and again to the topic of "the BOOK."

And thanks to those teachers who kindly allowed us to use quotes from their storytelling journals and emails: Sandy Anthony, Peggy Barnes, Joan Boyd, Tamra Bruner, Daryl Buchman, Kasey Clay, Robin Earwood, Tamie Enders, Vanessa Garrard, Megan Garner, Jessica Holloway, Jennifer Hulbert, Nancy Ishigaki, JonLee Joseph, Kelly Kennedy, Tena Kilroy, Angie Lavine, Rita Lenes, Ryan Lewis, Wendy Little, Kathy McConnell, Kelly McCarty, Jan Cote Morgan, Yara Nemri, Leann Onishi, Tamara Osborn, Anna Owens, Susan Ramos, Sarah Schmaltz, Allen Storkel, Kerith Telestai, Ines Zerbato.

Storytelling in the Classroom from A-Z

You can use storytelling in your classroom to:

Appreciate each child's unique story
Build community
Create confident, competent speakers
Develop rich and varied vocabulary
Explore concepts across the curriculum
Focus on standards
Generate interest in a new unit
Hone listening skills
Instill values
Jump-start any lesson
Kindle curiosity
Link content with emotion
Make connections
Nurture empathy
Open a window to other cultures
Play with language
Quadruple the FUN in your room each day
Refocus the class
Stimulate critical thinking
Teach to a variety of learning styles
Unleash creativity
Value the home languages of your students
Welcome new children to your classroom
X-tend understanding of narrative
Yield success for all students
Zoom around the world and back without leaving your room!

About the Authors

Margaret Read MacDonald has drawn from her many years working with children and her academic work for her Ph.D. in Folklore to write more than 60 books on folklore and story-telling topics. Her ability to retell folktales in a way that makes them easy for beginning storytellers to share has made her resource books, picture books, and collections of stories best sellers. Her popularity as an author has also led to invitations for her to teach workshops and perform these stories around the world. Her extensive travels and her years teaching storytelling for Lesley University and the University of Washington helped shape the concept for this book…which was envisioned by her daughter Jennifer.

Jen and **Nat Whitman** have made storytelling the heart of their classrooms for as long as they've been teaching. They began their education careers in Washington State before moving overseas to teach at international schools in Hong Kong, Germany, and Thailand. Jen is an early childhood specialist and has taught Grades K-2 for more than 15 years. Nat was a classroom teacher in Grades 2-4 for many years before moving to the library, where he continues to use storytelling daily in his role as a school librarian. In addition to their years of classroom experience, the Whitmans are also professional storytellers. They perform as a tandem-telling team in schools and libraries around the world. They have presented workshops on using storytelling in the classroom in a variety of settings, including educational conferences for the European Council of International Schools (ECIS) and the East Asia Regional Council of Schools (EARCOS). Jen and Nat continue to be amazed at the power of storytelling to transform student learning in the classroom, and they are delighted to be teaming with Margaret Read MacDonald to encourage teachers around the globe to teach with story!